To Rich,

"Well thou didst advise

Many thanks to a true friend!

Tom

The Birth of Popular Culture

THE BIRTH OF
POPULAR
CULTURE

BEN JONSON, MAID MARIAN AND ROBIN HOOD

By Tom Hayes

Duquesne University Press
Pittsburgh, Pennsylvania

Published in the United States of America.

by Duquesne University Press
600 Forbes Avenue
Pittsburgh, PA 15282–0101

Library of Congress Cataloging-in-Publication Data

Hayes T. Wilson (Thomas Wilson), 1940–
    The birth of popular culture : Ben Jonson, Maid Marian, and Robin
Hood / by Tom Hayes.
        p. cm.
    Includes bibliographical references and index.
    ISBN 0–8207–0241–2 : $28.95
    1. Jonson, Ben, 1573?–1637. Sad Shepherd. 2. Jonson, Ben,
1573?–1637—Criticism and interpretation. 3. Great Britain—Popular
culture—History—17th century. 4. Popular literature—England—
History and criticism. 5. Robin Hood (Legendary character) in
literature. 6. Authorship—History—17th century. 7. Folklore in
literature. I. Title.
PR2618.H39   1991
822'.3—dc20   91–34934
                                                                          CIP

For Lee Quinby

When other birds are still the screech owls take
up the strain, like mourning women their
ancient u-lu-lu. Their dismal scream is truly
Ben Jonsonian. Wise midnight hags!

—Henry David Thoreau, *Walden*

Contents

Acknowledgments

Friends and colleagues have sustained me over a long period of composition. Martin Stevens first told me that I *should* write this book and Bridget Hill told me I *could* write it. Angus Fletcher and Don Wayne read early drafts and encouraged me to overcome doubts about what I was trying to do. Stanley Aronowitz, John Dore, John Brenkman, Mieke Bal, Gayatri Spivak, and Peter Stallybrass have inspired and challenged me in various ways. I have also learned a lot from conversations with Charles Molesworth, Fred Kaplan, Evelyn Barish, Frances Barasch, Jacqueline DiSalvo, Gerhard Joseph, Mary Ann Caws, Peter Hitchcock, Lauren Silberman, and Tuzyline Allan. Joe Wittreich and Bill McClellan have provided good cheer worthy of the Tribe of Ben.

I want to thank John Shawcross for reading a penultimate draft of the entire manuscript and making many helpful suggestions. I also want to thank Albert Labriola for his enthusiastic reading of a rather unusual academic book and Susan Wadsworth-Booth for her helpful and sensitive editorial suggestions. I dedicate this book to Lee Quinby in acknowledgment of her invaluable comments on innumerable drafts. Without her inspiration and conversation this book would not have been written.

Note on Editions and Abbreviations

All quotations from Jonson's works are from the 11-volume *Ben Jonson*, edited by C. H. Herford and Percy and Evelyn Simpson, published at Oxford from 1925 to 1952 by the Clarendon Press. This edition is abbreviated throughout as H&S. I have retained seventeenth century orthography but have changed *i* to *j* and *v* to *u* where appropriate. Standard abbreviations of Jonson's works are listed in the first volume of the *Complete Plays*, edited by G. A. Wilkes, published at Oxford by the Clarendon Press in 1981.

Periodical abbreviations in the list of works cited are those used in the *MLA Bibliography*.

Introduction

A Popular
Apocalyptic Voice

... (to be an accomplisht gentleman, that is, a
gentleman of the time) you must give o're house-keep-
ing in the countrey, and live altogether in the city
amongst gallants; where, at your first appearance,
'twere good you turn'd foure or five hundred acres of
your best land into two or three trunks of apparel (you
may do it without going to a conjurer) and be sure, you
mixe your selfe stil, with such as flourish in the spring
of the fashion, and are least popular—

> *Everyman Out of His Humour* (1.2.37–45); cited in the
> *OED* as the first use of the word "popular" to mean
> having characteristics attributed to common people.

O nce upon a time, so the story goes, before the coming
of the technological revolution, there was a coherent culture in which people from all walks of life ate and
drank together, sang songs, danced, and told tales celebrating the triumphs of the past. But such a culture was
always already receding, was forever falling or already
fallen. Intellectuals and artists, those whose duty it was
to keep official records and preserve official history, were
blamed for creating a gap between those they served and
the great mass of people. But the exuberance and licentiousness of the masses were envied by those higher up

1

the social ladder. Thus, as courtly culture separated itself from ordinary culture, an ambivalent repressive attitude toward folk culture was created.

This story holds up well, owing no doubt to how easy it is to uphold, for it is protected by a mythology of presence, a logocentrism, that is built into Western metaphysics. By locating the originary repression of exuberance and licentiousness in the late sixteenth and early seventeenth centuries, after there had been hundreds of years of open spaces and more or less free expression, it is seen to coincide—along with sexual repression—with the development of capitalism. It becomes, then, an integral part of the dominant discourse—and thus of the ideological apparatus—of Western civilization. Under this rubric, exuberance and licentiousness were repressed because they were incompatible with a general and intensive work imperative; therefore, it was assumed, if one spoke and wrote about the exuberance and licentiousness of the masses in positive ways, one was engaged in a deliberate transgression against officialdom and was enlisting oneself on the side of liberation.

It is sometimes forgotten that what Mikhail Bakhtin celebrated in Rabelais's work was not a realistic depiction of carnival, but a discursive reinscription of what he called the *carnivalesque*. As Tony Bennett has pointed out, Bakhtin saw Rabelais's work "as exemplifying a *new form of writing*—without parallel in medieval literature" (Bennett 1979, 89). This means, Bennett notes in a later essay, that

> What Bakhtin celebrated . . . was not the carnival tradition as such but the direction in which that tradition was made to point, the specific way in which its cultural and ideological meaning was inflected, in being articulated to the progressive currents of Renaissance humanism. It was the *fusion* of these two traditions and the new meanings which accrued to the carnivalesque as a consequence, rather than the mere brute fact of carnival, that Bakhtin regarded as valuable. . . . Bakhtin's concern was not with carnival but with the *discursive rearticulation* of elements of

the carnivalesque in the culture and ideology of the Renaissance. It is thus the *transformative* aspects of Rabelais' work that he constantly stressed. There can be no question ... of any uncritical celebration of carnival as if the practices which comprised it somehow spoke their own meaning, voicing the authentic spirit of the people.[1] (1986a, 148)

Following Bakhtin's definition of the carnivalesque, I do not want to challenge this mythos so much as I want to redefine the premise—the repressive humanist hypothesis—upon which it is based. I want to do that by showing how the legends of Maid Marian and Robin Hood were "taken over" from folk culture and adapted for the emerging popular culture. How, in other words, with the rise of the middle classes and the spread of print, folk culture was simultaneously represented, appropriated, and marginalized.[2]

Scholarly interest in folklore is usually said to have begun in late eighteenth century Germany with the brothers Grimm, but Antonio Gramsci was the first to try to work out a self-reflexive theory of the role of the intel-lectual/artist in relation to what is sometimes called "mass culture" or, as I prefer to call it, "popular" culture. As Gramsci saw it, the central issue was how intellectuals and artists could locate resistances to the dominant culture and make them more accessible to working people.[3] Following this premise, Bennett has argued that both structuralists who denigrate popular culture as merely the means by which the dominant ideology keeps people in the thrall of capitalism, as well as culturalists who celebrate popular culture as the "authentic" subversive culture of the people, fail to see that

> the field of popular culture is structured by the attempt of the ruling class to win hegemony and by the forms of opposition to this endeavour. As such it consists not simply of an imposed mass culture that is coincident with dominant ideology, nor simply of spontaneously oppositional cultures, but is rather an area of negotiation between the two. (Bennett 1986 b, xv–xvi)

Similarly, following the cultural studies paradigm developed by Stuart Hall and others in Great Britain, Dick Hebdige has articulated a "neo-Gramscian" approach to popular culture that is distinguished by "the way in which it requires us to negotiate and engage with the multiple axes of both power and the popular and to acknowledge the ways in which these two axes are 'mutually articulated' through a range of populist discourses" (1988, 203). From this neo-Gramscian perspective, Hebdige later notes, "nothing is anchored to the *grands récits,* to master narratives, to stable (positive) identities, to fixed and certain meanings; all social and semantic relations are contestable, hence mutable; ... there are no predictable outcomes" (206).

In this book I have inflected this neo-Gramscian approach to popular culture through poststructuralism. The study of popular culture itself is further complicated by the question of what it is that is being studied. The phrase *popular culture* means different things to different people. It sometimes refers to the folk or peasant culture of the preliterate past and sometimes to the most current expressions of mass culture such as television, movies, and advertising. As Michel de Certeau has noted, "the uncertainty about the boundaries of the popular domain, about its homogeneity over against the profound and always reinforced unity of the culture of the elites—does it not signify that the popular domain has yet to exist, because it is impossible for us to speak of it without annihilating it?" (1986, 129)

But there is a continuity even—or especially—between the preliterate festive folk culture of the past and today's mass media popular culture. This is a continuity of the voices of rebellion, of transgression, of outlawry and perversity. These voices may be heard in the novels of Gabriel García Marquez and Toni Morrison and in the films of Spike Lee, but they are heard most especially in songs of Muddy Waters, Bob Dylan, John Cougar Mellencamp, Patti Smith, U2, and Tracy Chapman as well as in much rap and heavy metal rock. As Robert Palmer (1990), former chief rock critic of *The New York Times*, has recently written:

> The horrific imagery so central to the lyrics of dark metal permeates popular culture. . . . The world these bands sing about is not some never-never land of ghouls and goblins; it is immediately recognizable as the world we live in, with its gang violence, crack epidemic, threats of war and images of pain, in justice and repression. (1990, 31)

It is also, I want to suggest, the world of those originary outlaws Maid Marian and Robin Hood. Our awareness of a continuity between these worlds should teach us that the divisions of knowledge are not neutral, that, again in de Certeau's words, "any organization presupposes a repression. What is uncertain is simply whether this repression must always function according to a hierarchical social distribution of cultures" (1986, 136).

Colin MacCabe has argued that the point of studying popular culture is to show its "determination to break with any and all of the formulations which depend on a high/low, elite/mass distinction" (1986, 8). I am not sure that popular culture has such a determination, but I agree with Andrew Ross when he says that

> Intellectuals today are unlikely to recognize . . . what is fully at stake in the new *politics of knowledge* if they fail to understand why so many cultural forms, devoted to horror and porn, and steeped in chauvinism and other bad attitudes, draw their popular appeal from expressions of disrespect for the lessons of educated taste. (1989, 231)

In response to the need to recognize what is fully at stake in the new politics of knowledge, I want to challenge the parameters of my own particular disciplinary discourse by focusing on the inscription of various legends of Maid Marian and Robin Hood into popular culture. The debt I owe to Bakhtin's study of *Rabelais and His World* is abundant throughout, not only because, like Bakhtin, I focus on one author and one text, but also because, just as Bakhtin recognized analogies between Rabelais's world and Stalinist Russia, the way I view Ben Jonson's relationship to popular culture has explicit relevance to the role of intellectuals and artists today.

Jonson has been a key figure in attempts to define the "proper" relationship that modern humanist intellectuals and artists should have with popular culture. He was revived as a role model at the height of the modernist era when T. S. Eliot asserted that "if we had a contemporary Shakespeare and a contemporary Jonson, it would be the Jonson who would arouse the enthusiasm of the intelligentia!" (1920a, 121) Since that statement was made, Jonson has been both celebrated and attacked as a model for the traditional intellectual, one who "rose above" his questionable social origin by creating literary masterpieces—"high" art. In response to Eliot's reassessment of Jonson as a model intellectual/artist, F. R. Leavis revised his concept of the "organic community" in light of Jonson's representativeness as a humanist intellectual/artist. "Jonson's effort," he wrote in *Revaluation*, "was to feel Catullus, and the others he cultivated, as contemporary with himself; or rather, to achieve an English mode that should express a sense of contemporaneity with them. . . . In [this way] the English poet, who remains not the less English and of his own time, enters into an ideal community" (1959, 19).

In order to challenge this model of the intellectual/ artist, it is necessary to question the notion of Cartesian subjectivity upon which it is based. In the academic world, the field of cultural studies has initiated such challenges. But even in the academy, those who employ any of the various new theoretical discourses agree on little more than the problematic nature of such discourses. This is not necessarily bad, but it is confusing and disorienting and there are no easy solutions. At least none will be proposed here. Instead, what I want to do is employ an approach that borrows from all three of the perspectives noted above—an approach that is useful, workable, and, in so far as possible, aware of its own assumptions.

My chief assumption is that we construct our sense of who we are and what constitutes "reality" through language; another assumption is that texts—not just written documents but anything that can be taken as a representation or sign of something else—mediate our view of "reality." A third assumption, which follows from these two, is that any assumption about the intention of a text is always indeterminate. In other words, I do not start with an assumption that Jonson's texts are documents of either conservative orthodoxy or radical subversion. Such assumptions can only be made by those who attribute a moral, political, and cultural authority— a sacredness—to texts that I do not accept. It follows, then, that since I have no interest in trying to restore an original meaning of these texts, I do not agree with those who read these or other Renaissance texts as examples of how resistance is absorbed within a closed ideological system—a "new" historicism that veils an unresolved cultural determinism. But neither is my method formalistic; I believe a *dialogue* between Renaissance poetics and poststructuralist theory is not only possible but desirable.[4]

My motives in writing this study are all related to my desire to make a case for resistance to *any dominant view*, no matter how persuasive or politically "correct" that view may be thought to be. *Different* readings of any text—be they unique, particular, peculiar, idiosyncratic, or even perverse—are always possible. The task of unseating and dislodging the Eurocentric, heterosexist, elitist readings of canonical texts is neither trivial nor apolitical. Arguments for the relative arbitrariness of all readings, including the dominant ones, have important moral, political, and cultural consequences, but often those arguments require breaking the traditional rules of historical methodology, much as Nietzsche did in *The Birth of Tragedy*.

The title of this book evokes Nietzsche's because my

approach to popular culture is analogous to Nietzsche's approach to tragedy. I would especially ask readers to remember that just as Nietzsche did not attempt to locate the origins of Greek tragedy in time, I do not pretend to have discovered a historical starting point for popular culture. Like Nietzsche, I refer to an appropriation that, not incidently, calls up an emblematic image of birth. Chaucer's Wife of Bath tells us how officialdom—in the role of priests—intruded upon the process of birth; likewise, by showing how the legends of Maid Marian and Robin Hood were represented, appropriated, and marginalized by and for popular culture, I am putting into question another appropriation, namely the intrusion of the author-function upon the process of storytelling.[5]

Jonson's unfinished play entitled *The Sad Shepherd; Or, A Tale of Robin-Hood* is not as widely known as Euripides's *Bacchae*, the play that Nietzsche used to illustrate his argument, but *The Sad Shepherd* is a more interesting text than the scant critical attention paid to it would suggest. I want to use this play as a touchstone to anchor a discussion of how the masculine author-function helped create—and was created by—the rise of vernacular or "popular" literacy.

As is often noted, Jonson was the first professional writer, the first living *author*, to edit and publish his "works" under his own name in folio. Richard C. Newton has observed that "In Jonson's work we first find a poet appearing in texts which are decisively made for print—in texts proclaiming their own completeness, aware of their own permanence, and creative of their own context" (1982, 34, 36). W. David Kay has argued that Jonson's career may be seen as a "continuing attempt to interpret himself to his age as a writer whose individual works formed a unified corpus animated by his conception of the poet's function" (1970, 236). Several other scholars—Don E. Wayne, Timothy Murray, Michael D. Bristol, Joseph Loewenstein, and Robert Wiltenburg—have emphasized Jonson's "authorial propriety." But no one has explored the ways in which a genderized subjectivity is inscribed in the author-function or situated such a function in relation to the role of the intellectual/artist in popular culture.

I want to address such questions by investigating the concept of *legitimacy*. I choose this concept as my focal point because a large part of the Jonsonian mythos—the "story" that keeps his name alive—is that by legitimizing his role as author he became the model of the modern intellectual/artist. In their fascinating book *The Politics and Poetics of Transgression*, Peter Stallybrass and Allon White argue that "the notion of 'authorship' to which Jonson dedicated his poetic career was in every way in contradiction to Saturnalla, the grotesque, even to the theatre itself" (1986, 67). But Stallybrass and White do not consider the point Michel Foucault made in his essay "What Is An Author?" that the creation of authorship itself provided the opportunity for forms of transgression previously unknown—as the many imprisonments, fines, and ostracisms Jonson suffered because of his authorship of plays well attest.[6]

To reject a repressive notion of authorship for a permissive notion of theater is merely to reverse the traditional hierarchal privileging of Apollo, the masculine God of reason, over Dionysus, the effeminate god of excess. I want to deconstruct that binary, not just reverse it. Thus I want to suggest that the persona Jonson created —the authorial "voice" in the text—operates upon the tension created by these polarities. That is, Jonson's Horatian persona achieved its effects—one of which is to convince us of its authenticity—by *constructing* the very contradictions Stallybrass and White see his public career as opposing. As Arthur F. Marotti has written, "Jonson is an artistic schizophrenic, with both a Dionysian and an Apollonian side" (1972, 209), and I agree with Bruce Thomas Boehrer when he says he "would add that for Jonson this schizophrenia is necessary as well as convenient' (1990, 1076), but I am not interested in trying to establish a "correct" interpretation of the "price Jonson pays for his success as James's chief metrical syphocant" (1080).

I am interested, however, in the process by which Jonson built oppositions between Apollonian and Dionysian polarities, between the desire to restrain desire and observe the rules of good form and the simultaneous desire to break out from restraints, to overindulge and embrace excess, and, through this process, became paradigmatic of the modern alienated intellectual/artist. That is, I want to place this contradictory persona with in the context of the construction—or "birth"—of popular culture as a concept whose origin was coterminous with the spread of print and the rise of popular literacy. For as Jonson mock-nostalgically lamented in the prologue to *Epicoene*:

> Truth sayes, of old, the art of making plaise
> Was to content the people; & their praise
> Was to the *Poet* money, wine, and bayes.
> But in this age, a sect of writers are,
> That, onely, for particular likings care,
> And will taste nothing that is populare.
>
> (ll. 1–6)

The major readings of Jonson's career as an entity—as an *oeuvre*—maintain that throughout the texts he produced—as well as those produced about him—his multifaceted persona is in perpetual conflict with itself and with the social, political, and cultural milieu against which it attempts to define itself. I have no quarrel with this view, nor do I disagree with the view that this persona provides a focus whereby the words on the page—or the words spoken by an actor on a stage—are believed to represent or stand for a world outside the text. But I believe it can be shown that various disruptive elements undermine or threaten to subvert this notion of representation. Therefore what I want to emphasize is that success or failure of these elements in subverting forms of domination is indeterminable now as well as for the time the texts were produced.

Part of my purpose, then, is to show that the persona produced in Jonson's texts is built upon—represents—contradictions that mark the formation of an "alienated" or "marginalized" sensibility. This is a sensibility that articulates—even as it resists—the possibility of transgression, a possibility that authorship assumed in early seventeenth century England. In other words, I want to argue that the reversing of the binary opposition in which tradition is made primary and seen as the privileged concept, and in which difference, disruption, and discontinuity are seen as subordinate factors that need to be overcome, creates an opening onto the scene of writing—an opening that may displace the binary of tradition/difference.

The conception of an alienated or "split" Jonsonian subject that I trace in the following pages redefines—but does not necessarily contradict—Joel Fineman's claim that "the Shakespearean subject is *the* subject of our literature" (1985, 82). I want to supplement Fineman's thesis by suggesting that Jonson stands in contradistinction to Shakespeare, who established himself as a gentlemen with a coat-of-arms and whose lack of interest in editing and publishing the plays performed by members of the acting company of which he was a shareholder is legendary. Jonson's concern with establishing authorial propriety, his right to edit and publish plays as "his own" works, testifies to the perpetually frustrated ambition to legitimize and memorialize himself.

Despite—or indeed *because of*—this forever frustrated ambition, Jonson founded the first profession grounded in writing in the vernacular—as distinct from the legal and ministerial professions, which were rooted in learned Latin. For Jonson, unlike Shakespeare, writing was a commodity and an author was called upon to produce a form of labor that was inevitably "alienated," that is, an author had to construct a private self that was separate from the product and from the various communities of speech in which the author was immersed. According to the Jonsonian mythos, Jonson thus *created* the profession of author. And, in addition to rewriting, editing, and seeing through the press texts that he—to a degree unknown to us—had a hand in producing, Jonson created an identifiable authorial "voice."

He did this by appropriating the notion of the apocalyptic Second Coming, the Parousia, from its place in sacred texts, from Scripture, and resituating it in a secular context. That persona, that voice in the text, strives to convince us that it is the "authentic" voice of the author, textual presence that speaks to and for a troubled and corrupt courtly elite which, nevertheless, holds out an ideal value system that is besieged by the rising middle classes. The persona thus constructed is marked by individual alienation—an overwhelming feeling of isolation and loneliness, of moral repugnance and physical loathing, not just of others but of itself as well. This persona is always at odds with a subversive desire to strike out at— to defame and deride—the people, ideas, and values it is expected to valorize.

This alienation is central to the subjectivity of the intellectual/artist in middle-class society. Theorists of the Frankfurt School have demonstrated that through a process of depersonalization, middle-class subjects at the beginning of the modern era accepted and internalized the values of patriarchy as a monetary power rather than as a power grounded in traditional values. This, in turn, meant that the economic and social conditions that facilitated the acquisition of money were accepted as rational. However, this rationalized power is never at peace with itself; it is repeatedly undermined and subverted. In middle-class societies, this subversive impulse is an expression of what Freud called the libido, which is characterized by a desire to experience, to gratify, to reaffirm the existence of self through the senses.

In the discourses of popular culture, produced by and about authors who were interpellated as split subjects, this desire and its rationalization are contestatory. That is, this desire motivates behavior and challenges the boundaries between private and public spheres; it therefore needs to be checked and moderated. This requires either coercion, self-censorhip, curbing of appetite, or the interpellation of assumptions about proper conduct or "natural" behavior. And these forms of restraint are usually associated with the intellectual or "masculine" virtues that Freud said were created by sublimation. In early modern Europe, this excessive or unsatisfied desire erupted in carnivalesque behavior and marginalized discourses such as those associated with alchemy and the occult; these discourses continued to flourish on a popular level in various forms. In many cultural practices and genres, an animistic conception of nature and of excessive desire, a transgressive Dionysian impulse, was—and in some instances still is—associated with unbridled "feminine" sexuality and with hysteria.

Among the more challenging problems facing intellectual and artists today is that of how we can deconstruct the metaphysical assumptions upon which this opposition rests without privileging a logocentric and nostalgic alternative to a repressive and restrictive Apollonianism—without, that is, looking back longingly to a lost wholeness and harmony from which we have fallen. In *The Birth of Tragedy* Nietzsche saw Apollo as the god of illusion, whose realm is the world of dreams. Dionysus, on the other hand, is the god of

> the blissful ecstasy that wells from the innermost depts of man, indeed of nature . . . which the songs of all primitive men and peoples speak, or with the potent coming of spring that penetrates all nature with joy, these Dionysian emotions awake, and as they grow in intensity everything subjective vanishes into complete self-forgetfulness. In the German Middle Ages, too singing and dancing crowds . . . whirled themselves from place to place under this . . . Dionysian impulse. (1967a, sec. 1)

Under this rubric, Apollo, who holds out "the Gorgon's head to this grotesquely uncouth Dionysian power," is identified with culture, the shadows flickering on the walls of Plato's cave, the necessary illusions that make reality bearable. But in the Dionysian dithyramb, "something never before experienced struggles for utterance—the annihilation of the veil of *maya*" (sec. 2). According to this view, if we perform the transgressive act of lifting this veil, we will see the Truth; we will awaken from what Blake called "Single vision & Newton's sleep" and enter into a realm of exalted consciousness and visionary company.

Freud said that by sublimating these impulses—by displacing the sexual energy behind them—the Greeks "invented" culture, i.e. became self-conscious and self-reflective about their behavior and defined themselves in opposition to nature. But the question remains of why, now that we have learned to deconstruct this opposition, we continue to speak and act as though it were still an unquestioned "Truth." Why, after the metaphysical speculations of Kant and Hegel have been exposed as justifications for a patriarchal theology in the service of capitalism and imperialist science, do patriarchal discourses and practices continue to dominate Western civilization?

Perhaps this occurs because we continue to believe against our disbelief. We continue to accept the binary opposition between culture and nature, between Apollo and Dionysus, because the discourse that privileges the Dionysian as the "truth" of Apollonian appearance reaches us through the medium of a dramatic individual voice that is always at war with itself. The conflation of the legends of Maid Marian and Robin Hood exemplify this process that conflation brings together a representation of the heroic outlaw as cultural Other and a figuration of the equally oxymoronic madonna/whore doubleness of women as Other. The radical ambivalence of these constructions is the result of a cultural separation, a hiatus between folk culture and courtly culture that remains unreconciled in the popular culture that emerged out of this gap.

Therefore, before I directly address the question of how the legends of Maid Marian and Robin Hood are represented, appropriated, and marginalized in *The Sad*

Shepherd, I will examine three aspects of the authorial persona Jonson established in his texts: his Catholicism, his Horatianism, and his Dionysianism. In so dividing the Jonsonian persona, I do not mean to suggest that these are the *only* aspects that may be discerned in that persona, nor do I mean to suggest that they are mutually independent. They are, rather, mutually overlapping and interdependent aspects, three ways of talking about and reflecting upon that multifaceted, multivoiced persona that we, as readers and spectators, encounter when we read the texts that have come to be known as Jonson's.

My first chapter opens with a brief examination of a moment that Jonson himself privileged, that of his conversion to Roman Catholicism. I then provide a brief reading of Jonson's most famous play. *The Alchemist*, in order to show how, in that play, the debasement of alchemical discourse in a capitalistic world parodies, challenges, and empties official religious discourse of its claims to authenticity. I then show how Jonson constructed a Horatian persona that represents an *intellectual* poet constantly striving—unsuccessfully to restrain his *bodily* self from indulging his desire for sensual pleasure. Finally, my reading of the representation of Dionysianism in the courtly masques shows how the facile reconciliation of the forces of excess—African, witches, alchemists, etc.— places the hegemony of the court in question even as it seeks to affirm its dominance.

My second chapter explores some of the ways in which the legends of Maid Marian and Robin Hood were appropiated from folk culture and incorporated into aristocratic or courtly culture through the use of the pastoral mode, and how this appropriation anticipated the birth of popular culture out of the gap that opened up between folk and courtly or "high" culture. My third chapter shows how repression of the Dionysian in the mythologized world of the Sidney family estate, Penshurst, and how similar repression of the carnivalesque in the middle-class world depicted in *Bartholomew Fair*, undermine the ideal of the "organic community" and stereotypical notions of gender identity. Chapter four emphasizes the explicit treatment of sexuality and class difference in *The Sad Shepherd* and shows how the representation of phallocentrism undermines its potency. Chapter five examines the witch hunt in the context of the castration hysteria that it is produced by and that it produces. *The Sad Shepherd* breaks off just after Robin Hood returns to center stage with Mother Maudlin's broken belt—the symbol of his sexual conquest, his subjection of rebellious "feminine" sexuality. This visual echo, this *mis-en-abyme*, of Perseus's raising aloft the head of the Gorgon Medusa, is a metonomy of the Jonsonian author-function. At that moment Robin Hood's legendary association with the transgressive and the carnivalesque is blurred, and he is appropriated by and for popular culture and reinscribes its patriarchal ethos.

That tableau also epitomizes the dominant discourse's desire to establish hegemony and is emblematic of the ways in which feminine otherness is subordinated by masculinity in the author-function. Yet even this overdetermined moment of appropriation is not complete, not total, for the witch is still "alive," still able to threaten transgression upon the construction of individual (masculine) identity. These aspects of radical otherness—both uncivil and "feminine"—destabilize the assumptions that support efforts to appropriate transgressive desire and put patriarchal values in question.

In the epilogue I show how the Jonsonian persona, the Horatian author-function or voice-in-the-text that is Jonson'a legacy, was treated with profound ambivalence by the next generation of the English intellectual/artist. Some tended to trivialize the Jonsonian persona, while others—Herrick, Vaughan, and Marvell—began to construct a notion of the author, and therefore of the intellectual/artist, as a romantic solipsist, much as Robin Hood was seen to be in popular culture. My concluding argument is that the patriarchal ethos represented by the identification of the author-function with Robin Hood as a representative "beautiful soul" is being displaced in post-modern popular culture. Freudian and Hegelian theories about festivity—about theater and the carnivalesque—have been problematized. In a "high" modernist text such as Thomas Mann's *Death in Venice*, the contradictions inherent in the figure of the intellectual/artist—the beautiful soul—remain tragically unresolved, but in a post-modernist text such as Manuel Puig's *Kiss of the Spider Woman*, their irresolvability becomes so glaringly apparent that the humanist assumption of an essential fixed selfhood is exposed as anachronistic.

Foucault said that Nietzsche's announcement of the death of God "heralds the end of his murderer; it is the explosion of man's face in laughter, and the return of masks" (1973, 385). The murderer, of course, is Nietzsche himself, the author who recognizes that his presence-in-the-text depends upon a privileging of Apollo over Dionysus. When he sees this reflection of himself, when he deconstructs the metaphysical assumptions upon which this binary opposition is built, his face—the face of "man" —explodes in Dionysian laughter as it recognizes itself as a Medusan mask of the Other.

1

Jonsonian
Interventions:
Catholicism/Horatianism/
Dionysianism

> ... hath GORGONS head made marble of you?
> *Every Man Out of His Humour* (5.11.3–4)

LIBERTINE CATHOLICISM

I n his conversations with the Scottish aristocrat William Drummond of Hawthornden in 1619, Jonson privileged and estranged the moment when he converted to Roman Catholicism. He explained that after he killed his fellow actor Gabriel Spencer on 22 September 1598, he spent two weeks in Newgate prison awaiting trial. He was "almost at the Gallows," when he "took ... religion by trust of a priest who Visited him" (H&S 1.139). At his trial he confessed to the indictment but took advantage of a legal loophole originally designed to protect priests. He plead benefit of clergy, and he was asked to read a verse out loud from a Latin Psalter. He was then declared literate. All his worldly goods were confiscated by the court, and he was required to be branded on the base of the left thumb with the letter "T" for Tyburn, the place

18

where criminals were hanged, in order to ensure that he not plead benefit of clergy again. Thus Jonson emerged from Newgate prison as a destitute and branded murderer and—as a Catholic—still an outlaw.[1]

In Elizabethan and Jacobean England, Catholicism was often seen as sensual and theatrical; it emphasized the body and held out the promise of wholeness and undifferentiated pleasure. As is evident throughout both Reginald Scot's *Discoverie of Witchcraft* (1584) and King James's *Daemonologie* (1597), written to refute Scot's denial "that ther can be such a thing as Witchcraft" (xi), Catholicism was often associated with the occult, with exorcism, witchcraft and—like the theater—with the blurring of gender roles.[2] Richard Halpern has noted many connections between folk festivities and Catholicism; "maypole dancing," he observes, "defamed the Sabbath, and its adherents were dangerously prone to superstition and popery." And in such dark corners of the land as Wales, "popular affinities for both May games and Catholicism were rampant." "The crown," Halpern points out, "also recognized the connection between country sports and recusancy" (1986, 98–99).[3]

Moreover, as the material side of the occult tradition was taken over and developed into the empirical or "hard" sciences, its "soft" or spiritual side was consigned to the radical underground of "enthusiasts" who were excluded from the centers of power. These nonconformists, singly or in groups, maintained the system of metaphors and analogies in the face of an increasing awareness that those metaphors and analogies were no longer viable. Morris Berman has deftly summarized the relationship between alchemy and organized religion and explained how "the very intimacy between magic and Catholicism . . . led to an exaggerated emphasis on alchemy's esoteric aspects" (1984, 97) and how "Protestantism was able to undercut the soteriological claims of Hermeticism with the concept of secular salvation" (104). This split deemphasized alchemy's soul-saving aspects

while it emphasized the alleged ability of its practition-
ers to produce gold. Increasingly, alchemy—which, from
the time of Paracelsus (1493–1541), had developed close
ties to Catholicism—was looked upon as an anachron-
ism, a jumble of arcane pseudoknowledge with a decidedly sensuous popular appeal. By the end of the Middle Ages,
the discourse of the occult had become so closely inter-
twined with the discourse of the Catholic Church that
there were said to be correspondences between alchemical processes and the sacraments (Dobbs 1975, 34). Tran-
substantiation itself was viewed as an alchemical process
(Berman, 1984, 99).

One result of this mixture of occult and theological
discourses is epitomized in the careers of John Dee and
Edward Kelley, who presented themselves as geniuses
capable of producing gold and talking to angels. In 1610,
the year Jonson reconverted to Anglicanism, he used the
careers of Dee and Kelley as models for two of the three
main characters in *The Alchemist*.[4] Disdain for Dee and
Kelley was a result of popular opposition to the attempted revival of what Frances A. Yates has characterized as
the outmoded "Tudor religious and chivalric imperialism" responsible for "The uneasiness of James's reign"
(1975, 118).

As the title of Jonson's masque *Mercury Vindicated
From the Alchemists at Court* suggests, alchemy had been
appropriated by the ruling elite. This appropriation widened
the gap between the traditional idea of alchemy as the embodiment of a holistic attitude toward the natural world,
an immersion in nature, and the new experimental science
whereby humans distanced themselves from nature and
exploited it for financial gain. Jonson said in his poem to
Bacon (*Und.* LI), whose attitude toward the alchemical
tradition in *The Advancement of Learning* and *The New
Organon* is profoundly ambivalent, that natural scientists
had taken over alchemy's technology but had ignored its
value system. As Norman O. Brown has noted, the perception that "the sublimation of base matter into gold is the

folly of alchemy and the folly of alchemy's pseudosecular heir, modern capitalism," may be attributed to Jonson. At the same time, Brown asserts, Jonson saw that alchemy was "the last effort of Western man to produce a modern science based on an erotic sense of reality" (1959, 258, 316).

The dedication of *The Alchemist* to Mary Wroth identifies the play's theme as "the truth of religion," and explains that its author is "forbidden to speake more" lest he be taken for "one of the ambitious Faces of the time: who, the more they paint, are the lesse themselves." This locution, like the opening scene of the play, puts in question the very idea of a stable identity. The female figure of the infernal Trinity, whose members enter into a "*venter tripartite*" (1.1.135) to gull as many unsuspecting fools as they can, is especially fascinating as a phallic mother. She bathes, feeds, clothes, and protects Dapper and cleanses and purifies him of his "worldly pelf" (3.4.17), his filthy lucre.

Moreover, she especially parodies religious orthodoxy because, as a woman, her sexual practice inverts official doctrines about the purity of the Virgin Mary. And, since her identity is wholly determined by her profession, prostitution—which, in its total alienation of mind and body, hyperbolically parodies the business ethic—Dol epitomizes the ways in which the Cartesian separation of mind and body debases bodily pleasure. She is the obverse of the medieval nun, and in her role of public whore she parodies the Protestant ideal of the chaste wife as helpmeet. She therefore calls into question both Catholic and Protestant notions of woman—and the proper "place" of sexuality—and focuses attention on the way both of these models are determined by—and are necessary for the maintenance of—masculine hegemony.

Having internalized the business ethic, Dol knows that her most precious commodity is her own body, which she leases, never sells outright, to the highest bidder. And her obsession with saving both time and money, like her denigration of her own sensual pleasure, shows how, in the "new" popular culture, the Cartesian subject—based on the binary opposition of mind and body—inverted traditional religious values. What is more, Dol is also the obverse of the stereotypical whore with a heart of gold. As Edward B. Partridge has noted, "In modern plays where whores are treated more tenderly than Jonson chose to treat them there might be a certain wistfulness about one who refers to herself as Queen of Faery. But there is one here. Dol is ludicrous and vicious, but not pitiful." (1958, 125).

Dol Common is an inversion of a merry strumpet like Falstaff's mistress, Doll Tearsheet, who rebels against sexual restrictions. Dol Common outmans the men in her adherence to the "masculine" code of the business world. She insists upon order and applauds organization and efficiency. She chides the two men, who presumably should know better, for bickering like women and for not placing moneymaking above all else, and she denounces Subtle for his paternalistic claims of "primacie" over Face and herself. "The venter *tripartite*," she says, should be based on the biblical idea that they will hold "All things in common" (1.1.135). After Dol calls a halt to the quarrel, Subtle dons his robes and Face says "God b'w'you, sir" (1.1.197) as he introduces Dapper to "his worship" (1.2.9). Dapper swears by a faith diluted and clipped to the point of a meaningless oath that he will pay well to have sex with Dol, who, in defiance of Spenser's tribute to the virgin Queen and Anglicanism, is referred to as the Faery Queen (1.2.114ff).[5]

Since, like Face, Dol has no "genuine," no "authentic," self, she easily slips into disguises. Her greatest moment comes when she assumes the role of madwoman, which she plays magnificently because, having totally internalized the business ethic, she knows exactly what it means to separate thought from feeling. She uses the supposedly "respectable" language of the marketplace to describe their confidence scheme, and her speech is rife with allusions to the religious ideal of the original Christian community. The phrase "all things in common," from Acts 2.44 and 4.32, has several meanings in the context of the play. The surface meaning, to share equally, parodies the business ethic, whose more accurate motto is "every man for himself and the Devil—in this case Subtle—take the hindmost." Another meaning suggested by the phrase is that Subtle, Dol, and Face have engaged in a commercial speculation in stock, and a third meaning is the explicitly literal one: Dol Common is common sexual property into whom all men may put their "things," but only for a price. In this respect she corresponds to—indeed, competes with—the alchemical furnace or "womb," as it was called, from which the anally obsessive Subtle pretends to transform the base metal he receives from members of the Jacobean public, who are themselves, of course, "base."

Dol is therefore "common" in at least three mutually reinforcing ways—socially, commercially, and sexually. But her sexuality belies her commonality, for it is as sterile and as unproductive as Subtle's alchemy. As the reference to her as "Madame *Suppository* (5.5.13) indicates, she has willfully stopped up her ability to procreate. (According to the Oxford English Dictionary, a suppository was an object placed in the anus or vagina.) She has placed a barrier between her innermost "self" and the intrusive, penetrating, masculine world, just as she has shut off her ability to feel any strong emotional attachment for another human being. As an overdetermined, virilized capitalist, she is totally devoid of any feeling of tenderness or warmth.

In her parody of Elizabeth's role of Faery Queen, Dol chastizes Subtle and Face to "Have yet, some care of me, o' your *republique*" (1.1.110). As a personification of the (rational) mind, as distinct from the (sensual) body, Dol accepts the male-dominated business world's view of her—of everything—as a commodity. Her mind is honed to razor sharpness, but her emotions are blunted to the point of vacuity. She has no desire to experience the tactile joy of her body embracing another. To her, sex, like everything else, is a business, a commercial transaction performed solely for the purpose of making money.

Throughout the play, puns on religious terminology repeatedly draw attention to the ways in which capitalism mutually debases religious and alchemical discourses. For example, Mammon promises to use alchemical power piously (2.3.49) and alludes directly to Laski's relationship with Dee and Kelley when he says he will become "a *Count-palatine*" (2.3.331). In the next scene Subtle calls the Puritan deacon Ananias his Anabaptist (2.4.20) and enjoys gulling this representative of "the *holy Brethren/ Of Amsterdam*, the *exil'd Saints*" (2.4.29–30). He accuses him of being a heathen and a follower of Brent Knipperdoling, one of the leaders of the 1534 Munster uprising, because Ananias does not understand Hebrew words mixed in with his alchemical jargon (2.5.13). Finally, Subtle chases Ananias out of his workshop when he discovers his name, because in the Bible Ananias tried to cheat the Apostles. Like all sectaries he believes "All hope of rooting out the *Bishops,/* Or th'*Antichristian Hierarchie* shall perish" if his instructions are not followed to the letter (2.5.82–83).

Subtle's appropriation of alchemical discourse parodies officialdom's use of Latin, as does his "*heiroglyphick*" design of a rebus for Drugger's shop, which is based on references to Dee himself. Ananias says Subtle "beares/ The visible marke of the *Beast*, in his forehead" (3.1.7–8), an accusation Puritans made about the Pope as Antichrist. Tribulation Wholesome, the hypocritical Puritan pastor, believes Subtle's work may be used "Against the menstruous cloth, and ragg of *Rome*" (3.1.33) to restore the "*silenc'd Saints*" (3.2.38). Another obvious anti-Catholic reference is Ananias's objection to Subtle's use of the term "*Christ-masse*," saying he should instead say "*Christtide*" (3.2.43). Subtle tells Tribulation and Ananias that to defeat Catholic France and Spain they must use tunes and bells to deceive people as the Church does. This way they need not "libell 'gainst the *Prelates*" nor "Raile against playes" (3.2.86, 89) to win their case. But

Ananias resists because he hates all traditions. Alchemical and religious discourses "are *Popish*, all" (3.2.107).

The attack, here, like the one on the official grounds of divorce in act 5 scene 3 of *Epicoene*, is brought to bear on orthodoxy itself. Face warns Mammon not to discuss religion with the Anglican Fairy Queen "For feare of putting her in rage" (4.1.10). "And you must praise her house, remember that,/ And her nobilitie" (4.1.19–20), he warns him. When Dol appears, Mammon tells her she resembles the ruthlessly autocratic Catholic Hapsburgs and Medicis. Dol responds that his flattery calls his whole faith into question (4.1.72). Mammon says that Dol must not cloister her beauty in a nunnery (4.1.102). So when Surly disguises himself as a Spanish Don to expose the nefarious plots and tricks of the venture tripartite, the scene is set for the final confrontation between pretenders to religious authority. Surly-as-Spaniard (Catholic) no more represents the "truth" than does Dol-as-Fairy-Queen (Anglican) or Ananias and Tribulation as Puritans (radical Protestants). Surly's disguise indicates that no religious system may justifiably claim to know "the truth." All religions are, in the end, but "faces" or disguises, different ways of looking at, of talking about, some larger entity that exceeds all systems of human knowledge.

Even though Surly *knows* that the alchemists are frauds and goes to great lengths to expose their schemes, he does not triumph. He loses Dame Pliant to Lovewit and ends up muttering cynically about the need to cheat himself "With that same foolish vice of honestie!" (5.5.84) Lovewit mistakes poor Able Drugger for a follower of "HARRY NICHOLAS," founder of the ostensibly Catholic but nonetheless heretical sect known as the Family of Love. But Face, who has dabbled in alchemy, saves Drugger, the most innocent character in the play, from Lovewit's ire and apologizes to the audience for escaping punishment himself. Drugger's innocence—and his identification with the often reviled, despised, and outlawed Familists—complements Lovewit's emphasis on what Gerard H. Cox has aptly called "the primacy of pleasure" (1983, 85).

In *The Alchemist* the parodic use of alchemical discourse distances us from religious orthodoxy and enables us to see greed masked as religious zeal. The last poem in *Epigrammes*, "On the Famous Voyage," also written in 1610, achieves much the same effect as the scenes with Able Drugger; it links the ancient atomist with the contemporary one, Nicholas Hill, whose name is yet another reference to the Familist leader. This reversal, which draws attention to Hill's suspected heresy, undermines the official view that, just as the development of natural science may be seen as a continuous unbroken tradition of accumulating knowledge from ancient times to the present, there is a parallel continuity between the primitive Christian community and official Anglicanism. And this suggests, in turn, that if Anglicanism cannot substantiate such a claim, all religious forms and ceremonies are irrelevant. For of what value are rituals that are not based on a traditional tie to nature? And if salvation was, as the Familists had claimed, something that could be obtained without a state church, of what value was that institution?

The conclusion of *The Alchemist* slides away from a conventional closure that would leave the impression that such contradictions are resolved. We are left, instead, with an impression of irresolution. The play questions the relationship between spiritual discourse (the discourse of the occult, of alchemy) and the discourse of business—of capitalism, of organized religion—but the contradictions between them are unresolved. This irresolution is reflected in the Horatian authorial persona by which and through which Jonson presented versions of self.

HORATIAN AMBIVALENCE

In many of his texts, Jonson created portraits of himself in which he appears to be trying—and always failing

—to distance himself from the hypocrisy and greed that is engulfing the culture to which he reluctantly belongs. This portrait of the artist is based on a subjectivity constantly at war with itself. Apollonian restraint is constantly battling—and constantly losing out to—Dionysian desire. And, since this form of selfhood is constructed in a patriarchal society, a "normalized" sense of what society has set up as definitive "masculine" qualities—reason, decisiveness, profoundity—is seen in opposition to—and is often defeated by—aberrant qualities usually associated with femininity—emotionality, indecisiveness, and narcissistic focus on the body.

Jonson fashioned this "split" sensibility early in his career. In *Every Man Out of His Humour* he caricatured himself as the outlandishly acerbic—and therefore transparently disingenuous—social-critic Asper, and in *Cynthia's Revels* he appeared as the honest—and therefore radically antisocial—Crites. The self-portrait was more fully formed in *Poetaster*, where Jonson first portrayed himself as Horace, a beleaguered intellectual who, by exposing vice, hopes to make people more virtuous. This hybrid of studied reserve and cynicism emerges when Horace upbraids Lupus for ingratiating himself to Augustus (4.7.41–48), and is powerfully articulated when he rebukes Augustus for suggesting that he must envy Virgil's poetic gift as well as his material wealth (5.1.79–87). His soul, he says, "is as free, as CAESARS" (5.1.90) because he gives out his knowledge without charge.

Augustus abashedly thanks him for this "free, and holesome sharpenesse" (5.1.94). And, to cap off this portrait, the "Apologetical Dialogue" undermines the supposed premise of the entire play—that the exposure of vice will encourage reform—when Jonson says the purpose was not to draw a parallel between Augustan Rome and Elizabethan England. Rather he

> . . . chose AUGUSTUS CAESARS times,
> When wit, and artes were at their height in *Rome*,

> To shew that VIRGIL, HORACE, and the rest
> Of those great master-spirits did not want
> Detractors, then, or practisers against them.
>
> (ll. 101–05)

By repeatedly denying what he had so obviously done—
and the obviousness of the contradiction is part of its significance—Jonson called attention to himself as author, a
self that *stood behind*, even as it was presented by, a
Horatian persona.

Poetaster established this authorial persona; the ensu-
ing translation of Horace's *Ars Poetica* confirmed it. This
manifesto of the poet-as-writer opens with the trope of *ut
pictura poesis*, and what this poet paints is a picture of a
woman's head joined to a horse's neck, who yet presents
"upwards a fair female feature,/ Which in a blacke foule
fish uncomely ends" (ll. 4–5). This grotesque manifesta-
tion of the Terrible Female is an analogue to "That Book"
he is about to write; both are "like sick mens dreames."
Having called up these images in order to exorcise them,
the poet can proceed with his testament to Apollonian
restraint. He can now tell how a Horatian poet must,
above all, be a thoughtful *writer*, not a rhapsodist. He must
present himself as the perpetual outsider.

A Horatian poet must become an expert in *feigned*
madness, preserving detachment and not, like Empedocles, jumping into a volcano because of a desire to be
thought of as a god. For by allowing the self to reach this
point, by losing the ability to distinguish between feigned and "true" madness, between public and private selves,
the poet becomes a leech on the body of society. To reach
this state is to "be no more a man" (l. 668); it is not to
know "Whether h'hath pissed upon his Fathers grave"
(l. 671). It is, then, to lose all sense of *masculine* identity,
to sacrifice the sense of separate selfhood normalized
in humanist texts. Thus by recontextualizing the Horatian persona, Jonson defined an author as a man who saw
himself—and was seen by others—as part of a tradition.
The author's grotesque feminine texts, if ever they could

be properly shaped and formed, might do for Britain what
Horace's *poesis* had done for an earlier culture:

> . . . so mould *Rome*, and her monuments,
> Within the liquid marble of her lines,
> That they shall stand fresh, and miraculous,
> Even, when they mixe with innovating dust.
>
> (*Poet.* 5.1.21–24)

Yet there is a problem here. The assumption of a Horatian persona is a form of role-playing that, like acting, is
inexorably linked to the assumption that there is a "true"
self "behind" the mask. Similarly, the last epigram, "On
the Famous Voyage," as we have seen, emphasizes the
gulf separating an idealized ancient Rome, known from
texts, from contemporary decadent London, known from
experience. Another example of this may be found in the
"Epistle To Elizabeth Countess of Rutland" (*For.* XII),
which is modeled on one of Horace's *Odes* (4.8.11–32).
Here gold is contrasted with blood, acquired wealth with
inherited status, yet both are dismissed and the poem
concludes that only the muse

> . . . can raise to heaven,
> And, at her strong armes end, hold up, and even,
> The soules, shee loves. Those other glorious notes,
> Inscrib'd in touch or marble, or the cotes
> Painted, or carv'd upon our great-mens tombs,
> Or in their windowes; doe but prove the wombs,
> That bred them, graves.
>
> (ll. 41–47)

Again Horace's fascination with words carved in stone
attracts Jonson's notice, or, rather, Jonson's text foregrounds that quality of Horace's verse, which forces us to
focus on the words on the page rather than any image
that they might call up in our minds. The original aesthetic moment that inspires—breathes life into—the poem is
always already a part of the past. The muse, the feminine
aspect of the masculine poet, raises it "to heaven," where

it is inaccessable to mortals. Here on earth this moment can be known only secondarily as "our glorious notes,/ Inscribed in touch or marble"—that is, as a material *written* trace that may evoke the recollection of primary sensual experience. Thus, by a process of double inversion the poem "outdoes stone in the latter's own medium," for stone is *only* a medium, not a message. There were heroes, the poem reminds us, who were not immortalized "Because they lack'd the sacred pen could give/ Like life unto 'hem" (ll. 56–57).

Supplementing such a lack, a Horatian poet projects feminine aspects of the self onto the muse, which are then materialized in the "wombs" that breed poets who create poems inscribed in marble tombstones, but whose bodies turn to dust in the tombs themselves. Having thus established literacy as an arbitrary preserver of heroes, the poem asks a series of rhetorical questions that point to the idea that "only poets," such as Dionysus who "set bright ARIADNES crowne so high" (l. 60), and who are "rapt with rage divine" (l. 63), are able to preserve—and represent—*feminine* virtue such as that of Elizabeth I, Elizabeth, Countess of Rutland, or Jonson's special inspiration, Lucy Harington, Countess of Bedford. For her, Jonson, Orpheus-like, writes his "strange *poems*, which," in accordance with Horace's account of his own texts, "like a rich, and golden *pyramede*,/ Borne up by statues" (ll. 81, 84) preserve the "high, and noble matter, such as flies/ From braines entranc'd and filled with extasies" (ll. 89–90). The lapidary texts, then, preserve the creations of those boundary-violating fits of originary Dionysian passion by which poets reveal their inner spiritual selves to the outside world.

The next poem in the collection, the "Epistle. To Katherine, Lady Aubigny" (*For.* XIII), draws a direct analogy between Jonson's role as a producer of poems and Lady Aubigny as a producer of male heirs. Because the poet is required to serve the king, he has had his wit indicted. But he refuses to alter his appearance or abandon his "selfe" (l. 17). Instead, he praises Lady Aubigny's self in his epistle, his written poem, which is a mirror in which she may "see/ In my character, what your features bee" (ll. 23–24). Both Lady Aubigny and the poet stand on the margin of the phallocentric circle of power and are required to define themselves through their service to the members of that circle, which is seen as a form of payment (ll. 53, 96). The speaker, a Horatian outsider, tells great ones that now "they all weare maskes" (l. 70) so that "no man know,/ Whether it be a face they weare, or no" (ll. 79–80). Presumably there was a time when poets spoke directly and immediately, when there was no gap between their articulation and their experience, between their "true" selves and their textual selves, between them and their patrons. These times are now degenerate from those. But Lady Aubigny's pregnancy is a harbinger of better times. It will bring what is inside—the child—out into the world, just as the poet will give birth to his poem by delivering it to his patron. This child will be inside the ruling circle of the aristocracy, and so will Jonson's poem. Neither child nor poem will ever be an outsider, like Lady Aubigny and the poet will always be.

Such wordplay blurs social as well as physical boundaries. There is an alliance between the poet's feminine muse and Lady Aubigny, whose social duty is to produce male children to inherit her husband's patrimony. For example, the poem separates Lady Aubigny's interior self, her mental self, from her external body. Her mental self, like the captain of a ship, has learned to keep her body, like a ship, on a just course and has "earely put/ Into your harbor, and all passage shut" (ll. 91–92). Since she is sexually closed up, and is therefore inaccessible to earthly men, her "blest wombe" must have been "made fruitfull from above,/ To pay your lord the pledges of chast love" (ll. 95–96). This oblique reference to marital chastity and to spiritualized sexuality parodies Jonson's own role as the outsider who is allowed inside the ruling circle: the "priest" of art, as he calls himself (l. 101), that is, one who has no hereditary claim to be inside the ruling circle and therefore must do something to be recognized. None of his bodily selves can ever belong there, but the self he creates on the page can. His "real" self, his physical self, is always dependent upon someone's favor to be allowed to be there, and his poem is payment for that favor.

This makes Jonson all the more aware that while court intrigue is carried on through a series of deceptions and false appearances, beneath these appearances there is the aristocratic identity, the hereditary blood-tie, which is also deceptive because it too is not related to anything people have accomplished or any talent they might have developed, such as the ability to write a poem. The hereditary blood-tie is part of them, but it is not "natural," not something that comes from the inside. It is, or was, bestowed on their ancestors before they were born, before they came into the outside world of the inner circle. Ambivalence toward this is expressed in the Cary/Morison Ode (*Und.* LXX), as the "Brave Infant of *Saguntum*" (l. 1) withdraws back into the womb rather than face the horrors of life outside it.

In *Underwood* the humor is bitter, analytic, indirect. "My Picture left in Scotland" (*Und.* IX), for example, appears to denigrate sight, the gross appearance of the body, and textuality, in order to privilege sound, which is associated with spoken poetry. Instead of listening to his words, his "voice," his love has

> Read so much wast, as she cannot imbrace
> My mountaine belly, and my rockie face,
> And all these through her eyes, have stopt her eares.
> (ll. 16–18)

The wordplay on "Read" and "wast"—to read is to see a text but not to see the actual object being referred to, and a waist is also a waste, that is, wasted flesh, and also there is wasted effort in creating poems that are unappreciated and whose moral chastisement goes unheeded— emphasize the Horatian idea of written text as monument. These elements work to make the poet appear—indeed, to become, in the reader's mind—larger than life. His love will not hear him; she will only see, or, more accurately, read him, for he lives more truly in his printed texts than he does in his spoken words or in his decaying body.

This Horatian persona, this stoic sage who lacerates his body in order to valorize his psyche, suggests that Jonson has a self or personality that is autonomous and not a fragment of the prevailing ethos or an extension of religious orthodoxy. In *Ars Poetica* Horace codified such a distinction between the Homeric rhapsodist and the self-reflective contemplative poet who distances the self from the cultural ethos. In "An Epistle to Sir Edward Sacvile" (*Und*. XIII), this persona puts on a "cheerefull face" (l. 39)—thus falsifying his own sincerity—to thank his patron for a gift that will help him build the triumphal arch that is his life's work. The epistle, like many others, is about the poet and his relationship to his art. The patron is only incidental, a mere provider of funds. The established roles between patron and poet are reversed. The speaker does not serve Sir Edward; Sir Edward is expected to serve him. And in "An Epistle to Master John Selden" (*Und*. XIV), the Horatian poet sees his Parliamentary friend's book as his true self and admits shame for his own praise of unworthy peers, but, again, the emphasis is on self-reflection:

> Since, being deceiv'd, I turne a sharper eye
> Upon my selfe, and aske to whom? and why?
> And what I write?
>
> (ll. 23–25)

This playful exploitation of the distinction between outward appearance and inner reality continues in "An Epistle to a Friend" (*Und*. XV), where it is bad enough to see

> . . . supercilious Sir
> In outward face, but inward, light as Furre,
> Or Feathers: lay his fortune out to show.
>
> (ll. 19–21)

Such contrasts between outer and inner lead to the conclusion that "what we call/ Friendship is now mask'd
Hatred!" (ll. 38–39)

These underminings of social amenities, of established
values and the norms of everyday conduct, give the impression that the poet fears he will become part of—is indeed already part of—this shallow-witted world, and
knowledge that he is a part of it drives him to acrimony.
"An Ode. To Himself" (*Und.* XXIII) appears to signal a
resolution of the struggle to accommodate his private
morality to public chicanery. He bids farewell to the stage
and turns to the silent world of print as a means of self-
preservation. He will retire from the city to create a monument like that upon which Horace prided himself (*Odes*
3.30.1–6).[6]

Jonson's repeated withdrawals from the public world
of the theater to devote himself to the private world of
poetry embrace the Horatian idea of poetry as a monument to self-reflexivity. In "Charles Cavendish to his
Posteritie" (*UV.* XXII), the dead man says to his children:
"I made my lyfe my monument," and in his tribute to
Shakespeare, Jonson envies the "Moniment, without a
tombe" Hemings and Condell created in 1623 to keep his
rival's work alive (*UV.* XXVI, l. 22).[7] In "An Execration
Upon Vulcan" (*Und.* XLIII), he says the fire destroyed
most of his library, including the manuscript of his preface to *The Art of Poetry*, but just as Troy was rebuilt in
Rome, he vows to replace those lost texts.

Jonson stresses the worthlessness of his body and ex-
alts the supremacy of his mind, but the sympathy he
elicits for his body repeatedly reverses this hierarchy. In
reply to a poem sent him by the painter Sir William Bur-
lasse, he paints a ludicrous picture of himself as an aging
figure:

'Tis true, as my wombe swells, so my back stoupes,
And the whole lumpe growes round, deform'd and
    droupes.

(*Und.* LII, ll. 4–5)

Here his feminine body, his physical self, which of course we cannot see, has degenerated from the former masculine "mountaine belly" and "rockie face" of the earlier poem. This metamorphosis—like the transformation of the thin Greek Dionysus to the fat Roman Bacchus, like Comus in the masque *Pleasure Reconciled to Vertue*, and like Jonson himself—is laden with nostalgic longing for a former self and repugnance for the aged, effeminate figure he has become. And the connection between this grotesque body and the process of writing is further emphasized in the poem: "With one great blot, yo'had form'd me as I am" (l. 13), the speaker laments, thus acknowledging that he knows he has been transformed into his poems.

In the "Epistle. To My Lady Covell" (*Und*. LVI), the ironic contrast between physical and mental selves—the "Servant" and the "Muse"—redeems the portrait from self-pity. Just as we had been lulled into accepting an image of the poet as a fool or joker, we are presented with the argument that all this emphasis on the physical is misplaced. A poet is not a physical presence, but one who creates an enclosed inner space of pathos in the mind of the reader. The poet may in fact weigh "twenty Stone within two pound" (l. 11), but the poet's muse, which "can tread the Aire" (l. 13), will save the poet from degradation. The dichotomy between the physical poet, whom we cannot see, and the muse, who has no strictly defined physical existence but who can inhabit the body of several real female figures and who provides inspiration for the poems, points up the difference between the physical poet, who will soon die, and the literary work, which will live on. This was made explicit in the epigram "To my Booke-seller" (*Ep*. III), where he rests his case for immortality on his printed texts.

This separation between the outer grotesque body and the inner spiritual self exploits the naive assumption of a one-to-one correspondence between the living world of oral poetry where one can see and experience the presence of the speaker, and the dead world of print where the reader has no external reference and is therefore dependent on the text. Jonson's focus on his described—but not "seen"—physical characteristics and personal emotions, as opposed to events, encourages the creation of a sense of authorial presence. In the controversial "Ode To Himself" (*Und.* XXXIII), provoked by the poor reception of *The New Inn* on 19 January 1629, the emotional intensity of the lines belie their declaration of withdrawal. The assertion of disengagement is contradicted by the anger, which is generated by his awareness of his own immersion in the very culture he deplores.

The tension created by this underlying contradiction between the desire for the presence of speech and the absence of print repeatedly manifests itself in Jonson's self-portraiture, where presence is always deferred, always put off. In the Cary/Morison Ode, he pictures himself as an impoverished poet who refused to produce a "mass of miseries on the Stage" (l. 55) and says he meant only to express "full joy" (l. 87). Having fallen from the primary world of speech into the secondary world of textuality, he paints himself as "an old bankerupt in witt" whose printer makes so many mistakes that he has nearly gone blind correcting proofs (H&S 1.210–11). In "To the . . . Treasurer" (*Und.* LXXI), the tough exterior once again conceals and protects the tender mind. He compares himself to a town besieged by disease and want whose constricted

> . . . *Muse* not peepes out, one of hundred dayes;
> But lyes block'd up, and straightened, narrow'd in,
> Fix'd to the bed.
>
> (ll. 9–10)

As his body crumbles Jonson holds up his muse as his "real" self, a self that is created from words on the printed page. "An Epigram To My Muse" (*Und.* LXXVIII) explores the dialectic between a deteriorating body and a creative mind preserved in print. The poem tries to put a stoic face on a harsh reality by asserting that the poet feels secure—a sure sign of insecurity—that his songs will live "next to *Spenser*'s noble booke" (l. 24). If the Treasurer allows his poems to be printed—censorship was ever-present—his muse will rejoice because, "Being sent to one, they will be read of all" (l. 32). And in "An Elegie on the Lady Jane Pawlet" (*Und.* LXXXIII), he is transformed into a monument:

> Alas, I am all Marble! write the rest
> Thou wouldst have written, Fame, upon my breast.
>
> (ll. 13–14)

Similarly, the elegy on his muse in "EUPHEME" (*Und.* LXXXIV.9) contrasts the imagined "death" of his creative self with the decrepitude of his corporeal self and looks forward to the resurrected union of these two contraries at the Second Coming when, at a great feast, sensual as well as spiritual pleasures will be enjoyed without guilt or shame. The ode to Venus (*Und.* LXXXVI) epitomizes the relationship between the poet and pleasure. Paulus Maximus's marble statue of the goddess corresponds to the poet, who eschews sensual pleasure and sits silently with thin tears flowing down his pale cheeks because his "well-grac'd words" (l. 35) have failed to bring back his lover. Another translation from Horace follows, this one celebrating the return of a forsaken love, and the collection concludes with two brief poems, one which denegrates the pleasure of copulation (LXXXVIII) and one that praises Platonic friendship (LXXXIX).[8]

In *Timber: or, Discoveries* Jonson pictures himself as a thoughtful, reflective *writer* who has shut himself off from the decayed social world plagued by "the disease of talking" (348). He needs no eloquence, he says, because he is a scholar who lives and writes at a remove from the world of court gossip; he is a lonely learned man whose enemies, to add insult to injury, upbraid his poverty; he has a woman who "is my Domestick; sober of diet, simple of habit; frugall, painefull, a good Councelllor to me; that keepes me from cruelty, pride, or other more delicate impertinences" (1359–62). Jonson describes the process by which he internalized his classical sources in a striking gustatory metaphor. The ideal poet must

> bee able to convert the substance, or Riches of an other *Poet*, to his owne use. To make choise of one excellent man above the rest, and so to follow him, till he grow very *Hee*: or, like him, as the Copie may be mistaken for the Principall. Not, as a Creature, that swallowes, what it takes in, crude, raw, or indigested; but, that feedes with an Appetite, and hath a Stomacke to concoct, divide, and turne all into nourishment. (2467–75)

Extending this metaphor, which gathers force from its blurring of the distinction between physical and mental selves, Jonson says that his purpose in imitating Horace was not to expose vice in the hope that people would reform themselves, "but, to draw forth out of the best, and choisest flowers, with the Bee, and turne all into Honey, worke it into one relish, and savour: make our *Imitation* sweet" (2476–79).[9]

Yet, as Jonson himself tells us, he was an infamous gourmand weighing over 200 pounds, a prodigious consumer of food and drink, a man who broke his hosts' furniture and coaches, and a voracious reader and consumer of texts. Now this same "injester" claims that he, like the most dainty and fastidious bee, merely sips at his classical models. Such descriptions do not just celebrate the carnal; they also objectify entrapment in the body, in the mother. These digestive metaphors indicate anxiety about the autonomy of physical being, of the corporeal integrity that must be established in opposition to the mother in order toward off the fear of being engulfed and swallowed up. The poems I have cited externalize this unconscious fear of being helplessly imprisoned, entrapped, or enfolded within the mother and within one's own gross, distorted, penetrated body.

Indeed, the sense of entrapment—whether in the womb or in one's own body—represents an ambivalence about the self manifested in the desire to ingest the entire world, to take it all in and make it oneself. But, as though in retaliation, the body remains—or, more accurately, becomes—through all this stuffing, alien. His Bacchic body —like his mind—becomes bloated and distorted by being crammed full of poisonous material that he cannot disgorge and that he must therefore try to assimilate. The rhetorical excess, the grotesque imagery of eating and digestion, then, suggest an alienation from the imagined "true" or authentic self. They represent a fear of loss of control over the body and over the bodily functions upon which life itself depends. Thus, I agree that Jonson eschewed what Bruce Thomas Boehrer has called "the ethics of moderation," but when Boehrer says that this means that "Jonson's moral discourse loses its capacity to bring about change" (1081), he assumes an identity between his own moral discourse and Jonson's. This assumption is at once too easy and naive. Boehrer attempts to stabilize the meaning of Jonson's texts by attributing a conscious motive or intention to him and measuring the success— or failure—of those texts according to the extent that they can be seen to accomplish that monovocal intention. I believe, if we are to deal with questions of intention, that Jonson's intentions were more subtle, complex, and covert than Boehrer allows. But I am more interested in the *unconscious*, in what is repressed from consciousness, as a signifier of social meanings, than in the conscious mind as a *determinant* of personal intention.

BACCHIC DIONYSIANISM

In the masques Jonson wrote for the court of King James, this inverted and subversive opposition between the Apollonian mind and the Dionysian—or at least Bacchic—body is played out, but never convincingly resolved. That is to say, there is always something "leftover," as it were, some "excess" in whatever force is to be subsumed that is never quite subsumed, never totally absorbed by whatever figure is representative of monarchical power. Indeed, in his study of *The Transcendental Masque*, Angus Fletcher has observed that the disruptive Proteus figures who appear in many of Jonson's masques are surrogates for the poet himself. Fletcher describes this "demiurgic persona" as a richly ambivalent figure, "A Dionysian Lord of Misrule in opposition to the Apollo of the 'main masque.' " Moreover, he or she is "the most complicating sort of persona the masque maker could place at the center of his works . . . because without Dionysian metamorphoses no artful controlled music of Apollo would be possible, since the primitive precedes the artificial and constrained." And of course there can be no awareness that the Dionysian is "primitive" until and unless it is viewed retrospectively from the vantage point of artificiality and constraint. Fletcher's point, therefore, requires us to read individual masques in *opposition* to their generic intention. For while misrule is supposed to be fully contained so that "Apollonian law can take root in a living political ground," in the late masques Dionysianism approaches a "neurotic frenzy, in a cancerous proliferation of antimasque dances —but for good reason, since politics outside the court is getting closer to the court, and misrule is becoming a genuine political threat to the protected sacred space" (1971, 19, 21).

The conflict between Dionysian excess and Apollonian restraint is, of course, unresolvable, or, when and if a resolution is attempted, it is unexplained and unmotivated. And, further, this irresolution is symptomatic of the function of the author in popular culture. In these masques an idealized Apollonian figure, often a royal personage, appears, like a *deus ex machina*, and suppresses the desire for pleasure; or, alternatively, a Dionysian figure suddenly, and inexplicably, submits to an Apollonian one. Thus, in *The Masque of Blacknesse*, the beautiful, refined African women pair off with "the *Britaine* men" who "Invite them, boldly, to the shore,/ [where] Their beauties shall be scorch'd no more" (ll. 259, 262–63). But at the end of the masque the African women return to the sea, having "woane,/ In sight of *Albion*, NEPTUNES sonne" (ll. 360–61). And when in *Hymenaei* Reason triumphs over Opinion and Truth, telling the virgins:

"To *sacred* HYMEN, reconciled, yeeld:
Nor (so to yeeld) thinke it least *despight*.
'It is a conquest to submit to right".

(ll. 929–31)

This forced reconciliation represents a site of unresolved opposition and resistence.[10] Venus's inexplicable renunciation of her autonomy in order to marry Vulcan in *The Haddington Masque* and Fame's dispelling of the witches in *The Masque of Queenes* are also sites of unresolved— and unresolvable—conflict.

All of these masques were written *by* an outlaw *for* an outlaw, for all of them were commissioned by the Catholic queen who had not lived with the king for several years. In the last named masque, the leader of the witches rallies her crew—one of whom was Lady Frances Howard who, as we shall see, would later be accused of *being* a witch—by telling them Virtue's Age of Gold will return if they let their "native manners" corrupt them with ease (ll. 141–43). This expressed desire to revive the Golden Age evokes an idealized vision of primitive communism that ended with the introduction of private property and political authority. The Dame says that unless the witches actively disturb the peace, the masque's aristocratic audience will maintain its privileged position. As women who are displaced from the centers of power, and who seek to undermine those centers even though they are in some ways dependent on them, the witches note that if they are able to cast off their sloth they will

Mixe Hell, wth Heaven; and make *Nature* fight
Wthin her selfe.

(ll. 147–48)

Like exemplary entrepreneurs, the witches will employ the most unscrupulous competitive methods to achieve material wealth, and they will exploit their knowledge of the physical world to accomplish this end. For, unlike the aristocrats, they have no illusions about the fact that power comes from material wealth. In accordance with the established conventions of the poetry of praise, the speech may be read as a thinly veiled warning to the king, who prided himself on his passive foreign policy, that he had better take a more active role in preserving the power of his class. Surely this is at least one of the functions of the witches' cursing of "a soft peace" (l. 144).

The witches are only antithetical to the aristocratic queens in that, like Elizabeth I, they are all successful warrior women who are not subordinate to men. In the introduction to the masque, we are told that they, like the black women in the earlier masque, are "opposites to good *Fame*" (H&S 7.282)—that is, they have bad reputations in courtly society. On one level the witches stand for warrior women like Elizabeth, and the queens stand for docile women like Anne. But from Queen Anne's point of view—which was that of a Roman Catholic woman who knew she had been ostracized and knew she was considered to be frivolous and hedonistic—the masque could be seen to challenge the idea that women *should* be subordinate to men. For woman-as-witch is but another facet of woman-as-hedonist, which Queen Anne was often accused of being. In several ways the masque undermines the phallocentrism of the Jacobean court, decenters it and displaces it with a Dionysian alternative. The removal of the king from the center of the masque is the most radical component of this displacement, this subversion, rooted in what were presumed—indeed, are still presumed—to be intrinsically feminine values: privacy, intimacy, mothering, family unity.

In the passage cited, the Dame refers to "Vertue" as a feminine figure who through "her antique birth/ . . . will restore" Justice and Faith and "retrive her *Age of Gold*" (ll. 136–42). But when Heroique Virtue, modeled on

Perseus, descends from the House of Fame to dispel the witches from their magical dance in which they "do all things contrary to the custome of Men" (ll. 347–48), he is a masculine figure (l. 365 and note q). In an oblique reference to his legendary slaying of Medusa, he says he begot his daughter, Fame, when he "cut of *Terror*" who died "when *Fame* was gotten" (ll. 374–375). This sexually ambivalent figure then draws the courtly audience's attention to the columns of the House of Fame, which are carved in the figures of "Men-making *Poets*, and those well made Men" (l. 386). These men had to leave behind some memorable work, had to forget selfish masculine pride and become inspired by the female muse, Fame herself, who has, on this night, descended "to this *lesser World*" (l. 395) to honor the queens, "the choyse/ of Woman-kind" (ll. 410–11) who will," . . . after death . . . / . . . live aeternis'd in the *House* of F*ame*" (ll. 412–13) where they will hourly hear stories of Belanna (Queen Anne herself, who played the part), whose name is reminiscent of Spenser's name for Elizabeth I, Bel-phoebe. Anne is thus, in transparently hyperbolic words and images, seen to accomplish what Elizabeth I failed to achieve. Unlike the former queen, who forsook her femininity and became completely masculinized in the effort to remain invulnerable, Anne retains her femininity yet also becomes a true warrior *woman*.[11]

Throughout these masques, gender categories are repeatedly transgressed and their definitions are frequently blurred. Underlying and motivating this confusion of conventional gender roles is a discrepancy between two kinds of Dionysianism, one a "classic" form verifiable by reference to ancient texts, which was allied with the "feminine" (i.e., with marginalized rebellion against patriarchy), and the other a debauched or Bacchic Dionysianism that James was seen—or used—to represent. Indeed, Sir Anthony Weldon's infamous account of James's fondling of his favorites no longer shocks middle-class sensibilities, but it is often cited as evidence of his misogyny. This conflation of misogyny and homosexuality is based on homophobic assumptions about masculine vulnerability in relationship to the voraciousness of a feminine Other, assumptions that James's Bacchic Dionysianism appears to—or is made to appear to—encourage.

In *The Masque of Queenes* both witches and queens are martially self-assertive and aggressive while the men are, like James's foreign policy, passively submissive. Vertue specifically states that Bel-anna "alone" possesses "all vertues" (ll. 416–17), and the martial glories of this "Queene of the Ocean" (l. 416) may certainly be read as a rebuke, intended or not, to the "most royall, and most happy King" (l. 432) to whom Fame's house

> . . . can give no'increase:
> Not, though her loudest Trumpet blaze your peace.
> (ll. 435–36)

This rather fatuous compliment, whose surface meaning—that the king is already so famous that it is impossible to expand his renown—is one that only the most sycophantic courtiers could hear with a straight face. But other possible meanings, fully anticipated in the tradition of epideitic poetry, also fit the context: Fame (the ostracized Catholic Queen Anne) cannot increase the fame of her father (her Protestant husband, who had not spoken to her for years) because he is morally unworthy of it; or, more pointedly, Fame trumpets the king's peace because she must, not because she wishes to; or, even more harshly, Fame cannot increase the king's renown, even though she trumpets his peace to the world, because his cowardly policy of nonintervention will not work. Or, in a Rabelaisian sense, the speech could mean the queen cannot have any more children ("no'increase"), cannot procreate, even though she heralds the king's "peace," as in "cod-piece." It would be as pointless to try to rank the possible readings of this ambiguous speech as it would be to try to decide which of them Jonson intended. Logical reasons might be given in support of all of them.

That the king's power and authority should be defined

in what Stephen Orgel once aptly characterized as "poetry of so much indirection, so little clarity and ease" (1965, 87) is surprising only if we insist upon reading the masques as the expression of what we assume to be Jonson's unequivocal intention to affirm an idealist concept of order, courtliness, and grace. But we do not *have* to read the masques as the embodiment of a linear history of degradation from pristine origin (form) to shameful fall (content). Nor do we *have* to give priority to the original live performance and see the printed text as secondary and derivative. For example, in *Oberon* the Dionysian ephebe's passage from adolescence to maturity, from the world of women to the world of men, is incomplete. What this masque depicts, then, is an interrupted rite of passage. Oberon (Prince Henry) does not join the patriarchal elite; he remains part of his mother's alternative feminine (and Catholic) culture.

Similarly, in *Mercury Vindicated* the androgynous, Protean, Dionysian figure is not won over to the king's side; he simply professes such an alliance (ll. 190–92), whereupon Nature asks Prometheus to do something to show that she is "no stepdame, but a mother" (l. 209). In striving for perfection, for example, men have disowned their tie to Mother Nature, a sin for which she says they need to be absolved. Instead of looking to the heavens and attempting to play God, men should steal fire "from Ladies eyes and hearts./ [Because] Those softer circles are the yong mans heaven" (ll. 215–16). Prometheus says that not many of the ladies wish to be violated in the manner of Mother Nature, but she proceeds to contradict and challenge him much in the same way that, as we shall see, Mother Maudlin contradicts and challenges Robin Hood in *The Sad Shepherd*.

Prometheus finds this opposition hard to believe and says if that is their desire, women have changed a great deal since the time of Niobe, whose many children were killed by Apollo. At this point the women begin to dance. "*Nature* is motions mother," Prometheus reminds the

men, "as she is your's" (l. 242), and after the dance he
tells them that though "woman with her ills did flie,/ But
you their good, and them denie" (ll. 254–55). Again, in *The
Golden Age Restor'd* Pallas merely banishes the Iron Age;
the Poets must be called in to restore harmony. And in *The
Vision of Delight* Wonder's attempts to tame "Phant'sie"
for the king are also feeble and unconvincing.

The futility of efforts to provide a social framework for
the hedonism embodied in and represented by feminine
sexuality is starkly evident in *Pleasure Reconciled to
Vertue*. Here the Protean figure, Daedalus, explains how
the feminine desire personified as Pleasure is "reconciled" to the masculine need of restraint, personified as
Virtue. In the crucial scene, Atlas, "the *hill* of *knowledge*" (l. 204), gives birth to the male masquers led by
Prince Charles himself:

> *Ope, aged Atlas, open then thy lap*
> *and from thy beamy bosom, strike a light*
> *yt men may read in thy misterious map*
>   *all lines*
>   *and signes*
> *of royal education.*
>
> (ll. 218–23)

The royal prince, having experienced a rebirth akin to
that of Dionysus from the thigh of Zeus, may now par-
take of pleasure with the daughters of Hesperus, whom
Virtue

> now . . . trusts with *Pleasure*, & to theis
> she give[s] an entraunce to the *Hesperides*,
> faire *Beauties garden[s]*: Neither can she feare
> they should grow soft, or wax effeminat there,
> Since in hir sight, & by hir charge all's don,
> *Pleasure* ye Servant, *Vertue* looking on.
>
> (ll. 208–13)

Virtue, now feminized, watches her reborn sons dance with the daughters of Pleasure, a perfect tableau of the reconciliation of desire and wisdom.

In the first three songs, the women instruct the men. In the first the women are specifically told not to *"per-plex men, unto gaze"* (l. 264) but to allow them to learn from them; the second calls for the women to heighten the men's *"sence/ of dignitie, and reverence"* (ll. 285–86) and move their bodies in such a way that the men might *"wish their owne were such"* (l. 293). The third song tells the men to select a partner gently *"as if they meant not to beguile/ the Ladies, but ye howers* (ll. 307–08); then they may engage in *"Grace, Laughter, & discourse .../ for what is noble, should be sweet,/ but not dis-solv'd in wantonnes"* (ll. 309–12). By feminizing desire —that is, by having the women become the representa-tives of the social ethos and teach the men to control their passions and their need to dominate women; by having the women set themselves up as authority figures, as masters of discourse—pleasure-seeking is subsumed within the need for virtue. But the fourth song returns us to a shattering social truth. Mercury reminds Dae-dalus, the master craftsman, that he was sent but *"to walke with Pleasure, not to dwell"* (l. 327); he has provided but an ideal tableau, a momentary escape. Though Virtue's *"sports be soft, hir life is hard"* (l. 332), and the Daedalean figure must return to the hill *"and there advaunce/ wth labour"* (ll. 334–35). Virtue can never be truly reconciled to Vice, can never be *known* here on earth. In her solitary oxymoronic existence, she can only be observed.

Feminine virtue—chastity, sexual abstinence and the channeling of sexual energy into and through allegiance to one's husband so that he may insure that the children his wife produces are his own—is a fine ideal, but it is *only* an ideal, a desire, not a reality. It is a *"stranger here on earth"* (l. 343) and has its own *"right of birth"* (l. 344), which is the hereditary aristocratic idea the masque is examining, but only in heaven, i.e. *not* here on earth.

So the masque may be said to undermine the aspect of ideology that it may be thought to be supporting. My point is not that Jonson *intended* to place the idea of hereditary patriarchy in question, but that that is the inevitable result of placing that idea under scrutiny. No interpretation can restore an imagined pristine meaning of an original text or original performance. Logical contradictions within these masques work to unmake familiar greatness, to subvert the very intention they ostensibly set out to achieve. Indeed, the king's repeated commissioning of lavish masques is a sign that he needed to be reassured that his power was not waning, that his authority was not illusory.

I am not suggesting that we should attribute the fact that the masques expose problems they were expected to cover up to Jonson's authorial intention. But neither can the masques' subversiveness be dismissed as a kind of ambiguity that, because every text is inherently paradoxical or ironic, leaves room for different interpretations. The questions those masques raise cannot be subsumed in a premature rhetoric of closure that covers over the aporias between logic and rhetoric and collapses such contradictions in a theory of genetic form. To do this is to accept the stereotypical opposition between "men"—those who hold power—as rational, serious, and reflective, and "women"—those who are powerless—as emotional, frivolous, and spontaneous.

The field of folklore in general and the legends of Maid Marian and Robin Hood in particular intervene upon and disrupt the stability of such binaries. For example, when John Keats said in a letter to his friend John Hamilton Reynolds on 3 February 1818, "We hate poetry that has a palpable design upon us . . . ," he was objecting to Wordsworth's self-absorption and solipsism. "Let us have the old Poets, and Robin Hood," he wrote (1935, 537–38). In the poems on Robin Hood and the Mermaid Tavern, which he included in the letter in the hope that his friend would like them because "they are at least written in the Spirit of Outlawry" (538), he tried to move back beyond the tyrannical fixity of presence that writing encourages even while it prompts nostalgia for the free exchange of themes and motifs. These themes and motifs draw upon the archetypal characters and situations of folklore, a field in which, as Carol J. Clover has remarked, "there is in some sense no original, no real or right text, but only variants; a world in which, therefore, the meaning of the individual example lies outside itself" (1987, 190).

The idea of legitimation that writing encourages, the fixation of presence, the name-of-the-father, is dependent upon the exclusion of the illegitimate.[12] Legitimation still retains its patriarchal association, as in *King Lear* (1.2.15–22), in reference to a male child's inheritance of his father's name and property by right of primogeniture, a right that could only be insured by men's control of women's sexuality. To be legitimate is to be in accordance with established powers, to be central, lawful, sanctioned, and protected, things that folk culture in general—and Maid Marian and Robin Hood in particular—challenged.

Texts printed in folio volumes, like Jonson's *Workes*, which appeared in the same year and under the same title as King James's own collected writings, achieved a certain precarious legitimacy, but such publication did not shut down the dialogic process of interpretation. Print did not *replace* the theater as the central legitimizing medium in early modern England. It expanded the influence of writing.[13] The increase in popular literacy worked *against* monolithic, centralized authority, against the idea that there was one legitimate voice in the text. Thus, while Jonson, like other authors, may have disliked the crude heteroglossia of interpretation, he also knew efforts to control interpretation of "his texts" were futile.

2

Graft and Stock:
Folk Culture and Courtly Culture

[I] did not borrow *Hermes* wings, nor aske
His crooked sword, not put on *Pluto*'s caske,
Nor, on mine arme advanced wise *Pallas* shield
(by wch, my face avers'd, in open feild
I slew the *Gorgon*) for an empty name—
The Masque of Queenes (ll. 369–73)

P opular culture emerged out of the gap that opened
between the culture of the rural folk or peasantry and
that of the upper classes—the clergy, the nobility, and the
bourgeoisie. In his survey of popular culture in early modern Europe, Peter Burke has seen this separation epitomized in the changing behavior of the parish priest: "The
old-style parish priest who wore a mask and danced in
church at festivals and made jokes in the pulpit was replaced by a new-style priest who was better educated,
higher in social status, and considerably more remote
from his flock" (1978, 271–72).[1] Thus, as they came to
internalize the ethos of self-control, the middle classes
gradually disassociated themselves from, and therefore
rejected, the language and customs of the peasantry or
"folk." But, as the evidence of carnivalesque excess and
witchcraft persecution indicate, this rejection and/or

repression of elements from the peasantry or folk was never complete.[2]

The Sad Shepherd: Or, A Tale of Robin-Hood is as close to an originary text of this emergent popular culture as we are likely to find. It does not simply combine or mix elements from folk and courtly cultures, nor does it synthesize them. As a text—that is, as a cultural artifact —it is at once more problematic and, as I hope to show, more significant, than that. The ways in which it is problematic and significant may be seen when it is read in the context of pastoral discourse, the discourse by which and through which the ideology of the ruling classes was disseminated. From the anonymous appearance of Spenser's *Shepheardes Calender* in 1579 until the publication of Milton's *Lycidas* in 1638, pastoral was a major mode for the representation of the ideals and values of courtly culture. Pastoral exploited the contrast between the supposedly simple life of country folk (remoteness from such a life allowed pastoral writers to assume that it was simple and allowed their audience to accept that assumption) and the allegedly more complicated lives of supposedly sophisticated city dwellers. Moreover, pastoral's self-conscious archaism often suggests that ontogeny recapitulaties phylogeny, that the history of individual maturity reproduces the history of human cultural development.

Christopher Lasch's observation that "a sense of continuity in a society is exactly what nostalgia discourages" (1984, 69) and Donald Wesling's remark that the modern myth of the bardic is part of "print culture's nostalgia for oral culture" (1981, 73), are indicative of the ways in which the humanist ethos of Western metaphysics keeps being reinscribed as a fear of nostalgia. As Berel Lang has observed:

> The desire for a center and then for representation of that center, which has motivated the history of philosophy— is the starting point of the postmodernist diagnosis of that philosophical history. It is with this diagnosis, moreover—

the moment of 'rupture,' in Derrida's term—that the supposed will for truth or wisdom in the history of philosophy is revealed as no more than a disguise for nostalgia. (1986, 211)[3]

The rural setting of pastoral is always recognizable as a nostalgic imitation of an idealized past that never was. It evokes, as Humphrey Tonkin has explained, the world of "make-believe and childhood." And "the stronger the temporal pull . . . the more the pastoral *world* becomes synonymous with the Golden *Age*," which looks back to a time "when cities were unknown and nature was kind" (1972, 283–84). Furthermore, pastoral often serves as a means of modeling the past of the individual, and humankind's descent into Iron Age barbarism is often paralleled with the individual's growth into adulthood. Harry Levin has pointed out that in *The Shepheardes Calender* "It is not . . . the book of nature that causes the fall but the nature of books" (1969, 42). Levin sees what he calls Spenser's "myth of cyclic reversal," which moves "from experience to innocence and from world back to womb, . . . [as] essentially a fantasy of exorcism, a technique for wishing away the undesirable aspects of life, . . . an attempt to turn back—indeed, to abolish—the clock and escape from time and history" (45). In this context, the Bible itself was often read as a pastoral work, as a linear narrative that started in a garden and concluded in a city, thus reflecting an urban civilization's desire to return to an idyllic past. The conventions of pastoral reinforced this desire to return to the primary world of the mother tongue and the organic community.

It could be argued that Jonson's project of establishing authorial presence in printed texts was progressive because it strove to create a sense of personal identity—a continuous self—in the face of what was perceived as an increasingly fragmented and fragmenting social reality. However, there is no mistaking the accuracy of the observation that Jonson's self-conscious attempts to restore a sense of wholeness for his shattered, scattered, decentered self foster an illusory sense of continuity with the past.[4] To read Jonson's texts in a way that suggests that by recognizing this we have discovered or revealed something damning about Jonson is to impute a naive intention to him, unstated anywhere in his texts, and to chastize him for having that intention. It is to assume, smugly, that we know what his motives were and to assume, even more smugly, that he was incapable of understanding the political implications of his texts as we understand them. It is, in other words, to impute an ethical naiveté to him and to assume that we can escape from that naiveté, that childish sentimental view of the past, into a mature, adult, clear-eyed, and objective view of history. To call something or someone nostalgic is like calling them superstitious; it is similar to calling them idolaters or fetishists. All of these terms are premised on the failure of the speaker to acknowledge his or her own logocentrism. The use of such terms is based on a refusal to see that nostalgia is the inevitable result of the inability of language to capture its referent, of narrative to coincide with its subject, of writing to represent speech, and of representation to reproduce reality.

Like Horace's celebration of country life in Epode 2—the famous *beatus ille* poem, which Jonson translated (*Und.* LXXXV)—*The Sad Shepherd* acknowledges, even as it appropriates, the presumed vitality of an imagined pristine oral folk community. But critics have, by and large, ignored or dismissed the play, as Swinburne did, as "a pure fantasy . . . not crossed or chequered with controversial satire" (1889, 87). Twentieth century readers such as Anne Barton have echoed this retrogressive critical deposition by calling the play a "presentation of a lost world, an imaginary refuge from the threats and miseries of a contemporary society heading towards disaster" (1984, 350–51), or by noting, as does Leah S. Marcus, that it "uses nostalgia for the lost spirit of holiday to strike blows against overrefined taste in the present" (1986, 136). This protective attitude toward Jonson makes it necessary to state the obvious: there is no way of knowing what Jonson's attitude toward the English Revolution would have been. He may, like Andrew Marvell, have seen it as an opportunity to cast the kingdom old into another mold. He may have seen Cromwell as a greater thing than ought below or yet above a king, or as one guided by faith and matchless fortitude to peace and truth. And since these must remain speculative questions, we must be skeptical toward readings of Jonson's texts that tell us we should be pleased that he did not live to see the beheading of Charles I.

The Oxford editors aptly termed *The Sad Shepherd* "a splendid anomaly" that attempts "To graft the frail exotic growth of pastoral upon the robust stock of English greenwood poetry" (H&S 2.215). The play's significance as an exemplary artifact in the construction, appropriation, and marginalization of folk culture emerges when we consider the implications of the fact that the Oxford editors praise Jonson's pastoralism for the same reason others have criticized it; to them Jonson's anomalous pastoralism, its divergence from tradition, was a virtue. Jonson, "as no English pastoral poet before him," emancipated himself from the murky symbolism and smirking satire of sixteenth century pastoralism: "Mantuan and Marot, Sidney and Spenser, do not, as pastoralists, exist for him. Even Virgil hardly counts" (H&S 2.223). Jonson's use of the legends of Maid Marian and Robin Hood, they argue, is a facile substitution for "the Sicilian shepherd in his daily garb, pursuing his craft and gathering as he goes its chance boons of wit and mirth," and they see his use of folklore as an example of "cheery Germanic humour" that allied these characters "to the blithe natural gaity so soon to be lost in the regulation melancholics and despairs of the later pastoral tradition" (H&S 2.224). Therefore they conclude that *The Sad Shepherd* is as abnormal in Jonson's drama as in life" (H&S 2.227).

The Sad Shepherd is a more interesting play, however, than that conclusion would suggest. For example, a significant part of the plot of the play has a distinguished antecedent, Spenser's *Faerie Queene*, book 3, cantos 7 and

8, in which the witch's uncivil son chases Florimell to the sea where she escapes only to be captured by Neptune. Finding the golden girdle Florimell left on the shore, Sir Satyrane binds the beastly son, but his mother releases him and creates a false Florimell for him. In book 4, canto 2, we learn that many knights wear golden girdles in honor of lost Florimell, and in canto 4 "that rich girdle of faire Florimell" is offered as a prize in a tournament. The girdle itself is meticulously described in 4.4.15, and its history is given in 4.5.2–19: it is named Cestus and was made by Vulcan as a symbol of chaste love for his wife Venus, who left it behind after she made love with Mars. The ninth labor of Hercules, we may recall, was to steal Hippolyta's magic girdle given to her by Ares. This story, of course, has other analogues that involve transgressive sexuality, such as the girdle the Lady gives to Sir Gawain and the handkerchief Othello gives to Desdemona (which was given to him by his mother, who had given it to his father to "subdue" him). And the fact that Roman Catholic midwives made magic girdles for women to wear in labor (K. Thomas 1971, 73) lends another dimension to Lear's misogynistic rant:

> Down from the waist they are Centaurs,
> Though women above:
> But to the girdle do the gods inherit,
> Beneath is all the fiends
>
> (4.6.124–27).

These fascinating analogues suggest that a close reading of the "splendid anomaly" known as *The Sad Shepherd* might reveal something important about the function of the author, cultural change, and the construction of genderized subjectivity at the beginning of the modern era.

The first written text to appropriate the legends of Maid Marian and Robin Hood for courtly culture was produced by the vehemently anti-Catholic Anthony Munday,

who was lampooned as Post-haste in the anonymous satiric drama *Histriomastix* in 1589 (Dobson and Taylor
[hereafter D&T] 1976, 221n2).[5] A decade later Jonson,
then a Roman Catholic, again satirized Munday, who had
been rewarded with a court post for his work as an in-
former against Catholics, in an addition to *The Case is
Altered* (H&S 1.305–07; 9.308–09). There, as Antonio
Balladino, Munday says he is opposed to those who provide "new tricks" and "write you nothing but humours"
to please "the gentlemen," but, he says, "the common
sort, they care not for't; they know not what to make
on't; they look for good matter, they, and are not edi-
fied with such toys" (1.2.52–58). This passage illustrates a
sharp class antagonism among the spectators, an antagonism that Jonson thrusts before them in a pointed bit
of self-mockery. For the passage not only satirizes Balla-
dino/Munday's perfunctory methods of composition, associated with balladmaking, but it also castigates his arrogant and contemptuous attitude toward the public.

Balladino/Munday professes to be a man of the people,
but this is the sheerest hypocrisy: "I care not for the gentlemen, I, let me have good ground, no matter for the pen,
the plot shall carry it." "Indeed that's right," answers
Onion, "you are in print already for the best plotter"
(1.2.67–71). The pun on "plotter"—one skilled in writing
plays and one skilled in organizing criminal activities—
exposes Balladino/Munday's venality. The satire, then, is
not aimed at Munday's popularity among "the common
sort" or at his refusal to write to please "the gentlemen."
It is directed toward his willingness to sacrifice any belief for the sake of material gain, which belies his lack
of respect for his audience as well as for his craft.

The attack on Munday, like Jonson's other comments
on balladmakers (*Conv.* 475; *Nep. Tri.* 160–74; *Und.* XXIII,
ll. 19–20), may indicate, as the Oxford editors would
have it, that "he was addressing himself with growing
exclusiveness to the more refined class of his audience
who could relish the finer method" (H&S 1.306). But

these attacks also signify a desire to see the role of playwright as an independent, autonomous and self-respecting figure who stands apart from the prevailing ethos and who attempts to write "things like the Truth" (*Disc.* 2353–54), a richly ambiguous phrase. After all, Jonson would have known that Munday was widely regarded to have been the author of *A Second and Third Blast of Retrait from Plays and Theatres*, a 1580 attack on the theater that reaffirmed Stephen Gossen's similar attack in *The School of Abuse*, which had been published in 1579 with a dedication to Sidney. Gossen had published an even more strident work, *Plays Confuted*, in 1582. Here he denounced the "Dancing of jigs, galliards, morrises, hobby horses" and above all "Stage Plays," which were the "doctrine and invention of the Devil" (quoted in P. W. Thomas 1973, 173). Jonson would also have known that Sidney had answered Gossen in his *Apologie for Poetry* in 1595 and that Munday was attempting to pick up where Gossen had left off when he wrote that the theaters were the schoolhouses of Satan, arguing that the writing of plays, an "unhonest trade of gaine, hath driven manie from their occupations, in hope of easier thrift." Plays, he maintained, "hath alreadie corrupted" the entire city of London (Munday 1580, 122–23).

Finally, when he added the satire on Munday to *The Case is Altered*, Jonson would have known that Munday's most recent project was a dramatic treatment of the Robin Hood legend in *The Downfall of Robert, Earl of Huntington* (acted 1598, printed 1601) and *The Death of Robert, Earl of Huntington.*[6] Munday took part of his plot from Michael Drayton's poem *Matilda, the Fair and Chaste Daughter of Lord R. Fitzwater* (1594) and was also indebted to the anonymous *Troublesome Raigne of King John*, the popular *George a Green, the Pinner of Wakefield* (c. 1588),[7] as well as to the chronicles of Holinshed, Grafton, and Leland, metrical romances, several ballads, and possibly a now lost May Day pageant or interlude by John Skelton, who appears in *The Downfall* as the speaker of the prologue and also as Friar Tuck.

Munday's major contribution was to suggest that Robin Hood was an arrant member of the aristocracy who was rightfully known as Robert, Earl of Huntington. Munday thus provided the legendary outlaw with a title and a noble paternity. Dobson and Taylor call Munday's plays "unquestionably the most influential of all pieces of dramatic writing about Robin Hood." For while the chroniclers John Leland, antiquary to Henry VIII, and Richard Grafton, printer to Edward VI, had described Robin Hood as "noblis," Munday's plays "left a permanent impression . . . by elevating the outlaw leader himself to the peerage (probably if not certainly for the first time) as Robert, Earl of Huntington." From this time onward, Robin Hood would usually be identified with the nobility. Munday introduced the outlaw hero into a London Lord Mayor's day pageant in 1615 as the son-in-law of Henry Fitz-Aylwin, the first mayor of London (D&T 1976, 44).

Sir Henry Hastings, grandson of Francis, the "real" Earl of Huntington, was M.P. for the County of Leicester. He was a notorious witch-hunter and took the depositions at the trial of Mother Joan Flower, whose daughters were hanged for bewitching the children of the Earl of Rutland at Belvoir Castle in 1619—an incident that, as we shall see, is part of the subtext of both *The Gypsies Metamorphos'd* and *The Sad Shepherd.* But what I want to stress here is that Munday's mawkishly sentimental staging of Robin Hood's lingering death from poisoning bathed the legend "in the odour of sanctity" (D&T 1976, 222). Munday also divorced the legend of Robin Hood from that of Maid Marian, a legend that is older than the Robin Hood legend itself, and thus stripped the combined legends of their transgressive sexual component. In these and other ways, Munday's plays divested the Robin Hood legend of much of its identity with the folk tradition of May Games festivity and the carnivalesque. His plays did not so much *appropriate* the vitality of the Robin Hood legend as simply drain it of social energy.

Other, more subtle, forces were at work in such an appropriation. In his wonderfully precocious study of Shakespeare's use of folk traditions, C. L. Barber explored "two principle forms of festivity, the May games and the Lord of Misrule. . . . When the parish went abroad 'togather for Robin Hood' they did not need to put into words what they were gathering" (1963, 18–19). Barber further noted that a "village saturnalia of the Lord of Misrule's men was in its way a sort of rising; setting up a mock lord and demanding homage for him are playfully rebellious gestures, into which Dionysian feeling can flow" (29). Following Barber, but critical of his view that Shakespeare's staging of folk culture aestheticized it and negated its subversiveness so that it became "safe" and "quaint," Robert Weimann has argued that "medieval traditions of inversion such as the Lord of Misrule," embodied in folk plays and village festivals, "offer the most important evidence for what might be called a Dionysian tradition in the Middle Ages" (1978, 20).

The legends of Maid Marian and Robin Hood had brought together festival customs of inversion and dramatic representation in the folk play. Jonson's interest in combining elements from folk plays and May Day festivity in pastoral comedy is evident in the description he gave to Drummond in 1619 of the lost pastoral play he had written entitled *The May Lord*. This play had, as its subtext, the scandal concerning Lady Frances Howard's trial and conviction for poisoning Sir Thomas Overbury because he opposed her plan to have her marriage to Robert Devereux, third Earl of Essex, annulled so she could marry the King's favorite, Overbury's protegé, Robert Carr, soon to be Earl of Somerset (*Conv.* 393–401).

Further evidence of Jonson's interest in the folkore of the May Day festivities may be seen in the masque entitled *The Gypsies Metamorphos'd*, which he wrote for Francis Manners (1598–1632), sixth Earl of Rutland, in 1621. Jonson's relationship with this powerful Roman Catholic family dated from his first years as a poet. The fifth Earl had married Elizabeth Sidney, daughter of Sir Philip, to whom Jonson addressed an epigram (*Ep.* LXXIX) and an epistle (*For.* XII). In 1619 the sixth Earl's daughter, Lady Catherine, married King James's favorite, George Villiers, soon to be Duke of Buckingham. *The Gypsies* was first performed at Villiers's newly acquired estate, Burley-on-the-Hill, on 3 August 1621, in honor of the King's visit to celebrate the seventh anniversary of Buckingham's presentation to him. Two days later the masque was again performed at the home of the Earl of Rutland, Belvoir Castle, near Sherwood Forest, thus intensifying the connection between Buckingham and the legendary outlaw.

May Games had been held from at least as far back as 1473. People from local parishes dressed up like Robin Hood and his band and participated in processions and round dances as well as competitive games, pageants, and plays. Such pageants, imported from Scotland, introduced Robin Hood to a festive tradition that had been neglected in most of the early medieval ballads. W. E. Simone has noted that "About the time Robin Hood made his appearance in the May festival . . . ; he [also] appeared in the spring festival of Scotland" (1951, 272). This marks the point at which the legend of Robin Hood was conflated with the legend of Maid Marian (D&T 1976, 39–41). J. C. Holt has noted in the postscript to his revised history of the Robin Hood legend that "Maid Marian became Robin's partner in the May Games between 1450 and 1500" (1989, 192). David Wiles has found that "the morris dance came into vogue in the sixteenth century after the popularity of the Robin Hood game had reached its peak, and to a large extent it served to replace the Robin Hood game" (1981, 5). The research of John Bellamy tends to confirm Wiles's postulate of two separate audiences. He argues, for example, that "the *Gest* [*of Robyn Hode*] had its origins in the royal household although there is nothing 'official' about it; it was not written at the suggestion of a member of the royal family"

(1985, 41). The research of P. R. Coss confirms this; Coss concludes that *The Lyttel Gest* "is essentially a literary product born of local society" (1985, 73). David Underdown has cited instances of Robin Hood plays being performed at May Festivals in 1577, 1607, and 1622 (1985, 98, 56–57). And he later observes that Robin Hood games were still being held at Enstone in 1652 (262). The ballads and the May Games were mutual cultural phenomena, but when the ballads were put into print, the legend underwent several mutations, not the least of which was an increased emphasis on Robin Hood's role as an aristocratic outlaw.

Jonson's attempted amalgam of folk and courtly conventions in *The Gypsies* emphasizes Robin Hood's ambiguous position in regard to that particular mutation. As hunter and outlaw he was both god and beast. He was an outsider violently resisted by the king's men, but he was also possibly a nobleman with a legitimate claim to privileged status. As a kind of eternal adolescent, he stood between child and adult, and his overtly sexual relationship with Maid Marian, as we shall see, puts in question conventional justifications for the containment of feminine sexuality.

In this sense *The Sad Shepherd* reflects the ideological crises of the age, crises that Jonson had dealt with throughout his career as masque-maker for the royal court of King James. How could the desire for pleasure be reconciled with the need for virtue at a time when changing social circumstances were challenging the efficacy of patriarchy as a way of restricting, controlling, and repressing feminine sexuality? This was a question that the women in the family of the Earl of Rutland epitomized. When she had appeared in the lost *May Lord*, the sixth Earl's second wife, Cecily, had recently lost her infant son, Henry. (He was buried on 26 September 1613.) Six years later, Catherine, the daughter of the Earl's first wife, became gravely ill, as did Lady Cecily's second son, Francis. The daughter survived to marry the Duke of

Buckingham the next year, but the son died on 7 March 1619. This occasioned the arrest of a serving woman, Mother Joan Flower, and her two daughters named Margaret and Philip [sic], who had been discharged for stealing provisions from the castle pantry and distributing them to "bad company." The three were charged with having caused both sons' deaths by witchcraft. According to a contemporary account, which presented "on the Stage of verity . . . the late wofull Tragedy of the *Right Honourable* the *Earle* of *Rutlands* children," Mother Flower died of strangulation after saying that if she were guilty she wished the bread she ate would choke her. Her daughters pled guilty to sorcery and testified that "both the Earl and his Countess were brought into their snares, as they imagined, and indeed determined to keep them from having any more children." These two young women were executed on 11 March 1619.[8]

Two years later another case of witchmania surfaced in Edmonton with the trial and subsequent hanging of Mother Elizabeth Sawyer on 19 April 1921. Henry Goodhole, the minister who attended her, immediately published her confession. The play *The Witch of Edmonton*, by William Rowley, Thomas Dekker, and John Ford —which features much morris dancing and two appearances by Maid Marian—was acted at Whitehall on 29 December 1621. But Etta Soiref Onat has suggested that this may not have been its first appearance (1980, 161). All of these events—and texts—are part of the text—and performance—of *The Gypsies* as well as *The Sad Shepherd*.

In *The Gypsies* the noble performers present themselves as members of a roving band of gypsies or outlaws, similar to that of the legendary Robin Hood, who transform gloom into happiness. Julia Briggs has remarked that "the masque breaks all the normal rules of decorum in presenting noblemen as a band of rogues and outcasts" (1983, 154). But that was precisely the social function of masques. As Dale B. J. Randall has shown, gypsies were often associated with witchcraft (1975, 86), and *The Gypsies* is an allegory of—and a thinly veiled satirical attack on—Buckingham's corrupt practices. Such carnivalesque playing at radical chic on the part of the aristocracy was not unprecedented. In 1510 Henry VIII's "Maying" took the form of entering the Queen's chamber with 11 nobles dressed "like outlawes, or Robyn Hodes men." In May 1515 he was entertained by 200 yeomen "clothed all in grene" led by "Robyn Hood" who invited them "into the grene wood . . . to se how the outlawes lyve," to dine on venison, and to meet Lady May (D&T 1976, 42). And in 1559 Queen Elizabeth attended a May game that included morris dancing and figures dressed as Robin Hood and Maid Marian (Stallybrass 1985, 137).

A hundred years later the gap between folk and courtly cultures had widened to such an extent that Jonson had to use Thomas Harman's *Caveat or Warning for Common Cursetors vulgarely called Vagabondes* (1567) to learn the argot of the underworld (H&S 7.615). Even with his broad social background and intimate knowledge of London street-life, Jonson could not rely on firsthand experience for the speech of the lower classes. He wanted to get it right. Rather than sneering at such language or making a feeble effort to mimic it, he went to the trouble to look up specific words and phrases and use them before the most exclusive audience possible. Why? Who could possibly have appreciated such precision? Surely not the lords and ladies who participated in and attended the masque. But Jonson was a marginal figure in relation to both folk and courtly cultures. His position as an author distanced him from any specific class or culture and placed him in a position to see language as a marker of social position. Thus the lords' and ladies' imitation of the speech of the underworld detracts from any sense of inherent difference between aristocrat and commoner.

The Gypsies exhibits familiarity with folk pastimes such as the morris dances, in which Maid Marian was played by a man "trimly dressed up in a cast gown and a

kercher of Dame Lawson's, his face handsomely muffled
with a diaper-napkin to cover his beard" (quoted in Wiles
1981, 5). Gossen and Munday, among others, objected to
such reversals of sex roles and attacked the entire institution of the theater because the presentation of stage-
plays tended to confuse gender identity and undermine
established patriarchal authority.[9] But Jonson's text posi-
tively revels in such gender-blurring. In *The Gypsies* Clod
remarks that the figures "should be Morris dancers by
theire gingle, but they have no Napkins." "No, nor Hobby
horse," replies Cockrell. "O," says Clod, "he is often forgotten, that's no rule; but there is no Maid-marrian nor
ffrier amongst them, wch is the surer marke" (ll. 738–43).

As Natalie Zemon Davis has noted, Maid Marian is the
most important English example of the ritual and magical function of sexual inversion. When she presided with
Robin Hood over the May Games, she "was sometimes
a real female and sometimes a disguised male" whose
"gestures or costume might be licentious" (1975, 137–38).
According to Peter Stallybrass, "Only in the high literary tradition did Marion [sic] become a chaste damsel; in
the popular tradition, she was 'a smurkynge wench' and
'none of those coy dames' (D&T 1976, 42), exchanging
lewd jokes with the Fool" (Stallybrass 1985, 122–23). Ian
Donaldson has argued that the charivari-like scene in
Epicoene celebrates sexual inversion (1970, 35–45). But
this celebratory mode marks an unease, for as Linda Woodbridge has observed, transvestism manifests patriarchal
society's fear of feminine sexuality. Nevertheless, at the
risk of pointing out the obvious, I would like to note that
Marian and Robin are both names given to both men
and women.

These themes undermined the stability of gender categories. For example, in *Robin Hood and the Bishop*, published sometime between 1620 and 1655, carnivalesque
transvestism radically subverts gender stereotypes. In another ballad, *A Famous Battle Between Robin Hood and
Maid Marian*, Marian disguises herself "like a page," takes

up "quiver and bow, sword, buckler, and all," and goes into the forest in search of Robin Hood, who has been ostracized from the courtly world. They meet, but since Robin Hood is also disguised, they do not recognize each other and begin fighting. Robin Hood's face runs with blood, but when he wounds Maid Marian he cries out for her to cease fighting and become "one of my string,/ To range in the wood with bold Robin Hood,/ And hear the sweet nightingall sing." Upon hearing his voice, Maid Marian recognizes Robin Hood and casts off her disguise. They make love and celebrate their reunion with a feast "in a shaded bower,/ Where venison is sweet ... [and]/ Great flaggons of wine were set on board." They decide to live together in the forest apart from courtly society "With all their yoemen gay," and to live "by their hands, without and lands" (D&T 1976, 177–78).

There is nothing of this subversive festival spirit in Munday's Robin Hood plays. They merely testify to the premise that those who inherit land are worthy to hold positions of power and authority, but those who strive to attain those positions through amassing wealth are not. In *The Downfall* the Sheriff of Nottingham is a cottager's son who was a clerk and a steward before he became a justice of the peace and became wealthy by racking rents. Robin Hood's murderer is another social climber who was knighted during civil war. Only Robin Hood himself is a true-born aristocrat who temporarily enters the greenwood to escape the cares of a bourgeois world.

Jonson's *Gypsies* likewise expands upon the sources of folklore in support of the ruling class. For example, Cock-Lorell (or Cook-Lorel), who is mentioned by Wynken de Worde in *Cocke Lorelles Bote* (c. 1515) as a captain who summoned people aboard his ship of rogues[10] and who is called a notorious knave by Robert Copland in *The Hye Way to the Spyttle House* (c. 1530), is cast as the first lord of the gypsies—the part played by the Duke of Buckingham himself. His songster sings a traditional four-stress accentual ballad for him in the style of those in the Robin Hood cycle (H&S 10.629). The song is about his dinner with the devil, during which they dine on a Puritan, a fat usurer, a lawyer, two sheriffs, a mayor, an overgrown justice of the peace, a jailer, and two aldermen (ll. 1062–137). But some 15 years later in *The Sad Shepherd*, this figure becomes simply "Lorel, the rude," son of Maudlin, "the Witch of Paplewick," who also appeared briefly in *The Gypsies* (l. 818).

These texts suggest that as the ruling courtly elite was increasingly challenged by the rising middle classes, it was identified ever more closely with folk culture. This accounts for the fact that, as Jonas Barish has observed, "verse reigns undisputed in the last comedies" (1970, 249). In other words, Jonson abandoned the practice he had done so much to develop in his early years as a playwright the attempt to make the language of his characters conform to the actual cadences of everyday speech. The new mass medium—journalism—may have influenced Jonson's decision to cease trying to imitate spoken intonation.

For example, what Anne Barton has called the "striking reversal of that trend towards greater naturalism" (1984, 238) in the later comedies is evident in *The Staple of News*, which extends a premise from the masque *News From the New World Discovered in the Moon* where the Factor says he hopes to found a clearing house where all information will first be brought and processed into news before it is dispensed to the common people. This will, supposedly, avoid the distortions imposed on it by those who print and sell ballads under figurative and fanciful names such as "the serpent in *Sussex*, or the witches bidding the Devill to dinner at *Derbie*." But the Printer has too profound an awareness of cultural relativism to swallow this; he replies: "Sir, that's all one, they were made for the common people; and why should not that ha' their pleasure in beleeving of lies are made for them, as you have in *Paules* that made 'hem for your selves?" (ll. 45–55).

Why should they not indeed? In *The Staple of News*
Peni-boy Jr. replies cynically but honestly to Cymbal's
similar inquiry:

> Why, me thinkes Sir, if the honest common
>   people
> Will be abus'd, why should not they ha' their
>   pleasure,
> In the believing Lyes, are made for them;
> As you i' th *Office*, making them your selves?
>
> (1.5.42–45)

Here the phrasing is nearly the same, but the play casts
what was prose into poetry. The masque, written for an
aristocratic audience, imitates everyday speech patterns
and therefore stresses the meaning of the words, the content of the utterance; but the play, composed for a more
general audience, calls attention to the words themselves,
thus emphasizing the language, the form or means by
which meaning is conveyed or transmitted. Unsurprising-
ly, the Prologue for the Stage expresses the wish that the
audience "... were come to heare, not see a Play" (l. 2),
and the speaker assures them that the author wishes to
improve their sensibilities:

> ... he'ld have you wise,
> Much rather by your eares, then by your eyes.
>
> (ll. 5–6)

In the play a whole series of special vocabularies are
lampooned. This may mean that Jonson was revolted by
the debased urban world where print journalism flourish-
ed and sought to show an alternative older agrarian world
of the countryside, a world epitomized by the legend of
Robin Hood and his merry men. Such a view is evident
in the second act of *The Staple of News* where the native American noble Princess Pocahantas is slandered by
greedy businessmen (2.5.121–24; 2.Inter.40–45). But the
way in which attention is continually drawn to language
throughout the play tends to undermine the assumed

moral imperative of its surface meaning. That is, we *hear* something quite different from what we see, and this something tells us not to trust appearances. The attempt "to graft the frail exotic growth of pastoral upon the robust stock of English greenwood poetry" implies a problematic relationship between two discourses, two ideologies. What was the expected hybrid? And do not the parasitic implications of the metaphor itself, which J. Hillis Miller has deconstructed in his well-known essay on "The Critic as Host," call attention to the difference between two unequal branches, the stock and the scion, the one firmly rooted in the past, in oral folk culture, and the other, "the frail exotic growth of [courtly] pastoral" parasitically grafted on to the former in hope of receiving sustenance from it?

But in at least one respect the figure is apt. Greenwood poetry was indeed rooted in England's agrarian past; the "rymes of Robyn Hood" are referred to in *Piers Plowman* (B Text. Passus V, 402), usually dated around 1377. But in works written in the 1630s pastoral is no "frail exotic growth," nor is the Robin Hood legend a "robust stock." Quite the contrary. In 1631–32 the tavernkeeper and ballad-monger Martin Parker published a synthesis of the current broadside literature entitled *A True Tale of Robbin Hood*, which, following Munday, stressed the outlaw's spurious aristocratic background and expunged the comic aspect found in the older tales (D&T 1976, 188). Parker's account neutralized the radical political potential of the Robin Hood legend by historicizing him and setting him firmly in the past. However, the 1634 fragment of a play based on the ballad *Robin Hood and the Potter* restored some of the legendary outlaw's transgressive political significance by depicting him as a sexually unrestrained vagabond who calls the potter a cuckold and smashes his wares.

The political and cultural significance of an anonymous play about Robin Hood and the Yorkshire yeoman of its title, *George a Greene*, which was still being performed in London in the 1630s, is more difficult to assess. This play re-presented certain aspects of the Tudor myth, which the court of Charles I wished to revise and relegitimize. The play is set during the interrupted reign of Edward IV (1461–70, 1471–83), who succeeded to the Yorkish leadership after his father's death in Wakefield, deposed Henry VI, and established the absolutist precedents employed by the Tudors. George a Green pretends to join forces with the rebellious Earl of Kendal [Henry VI], who says he is fighting "for the poore that is opprest by wrong" (ll. 586–87). But just as the audience is led to sympathize with this seemingly laudable revolutionary figure, their expectations are undermined when George tricks Kendall, captures him, and subdues the invading Scottish King James. He then defeats Kendall's loyal supporters Will Scarlett, Much the Miller's son, and Robin Hood himself in hand-to-hand combat. Then, having gained Robin Hood's support for the Yorkist leader, who represents established authority and tradition, he ambushes and beats "base-minded peasants, worthlesse to be men!" (l. 1150) The battle won, George welcomes Robin Hood and King Edward himself to his humble home. He serves them ale and declares that while he is "ill-nurtured" and "blunt of Speech; And litle skild in court or such quaint fashions," he believes that "nature teacheth us duetie to our king" (ll. 1186–89).

As the gap between the "truth" presented by such plays and the perceived "reality" of everyday experience widened, intellectuals—who were of necessity allied with the court culture and the system of patronage—expressed various forms of alienation from that culture. Martin Butler has explained this phenomenon by suggesting that the world of Charles I "was still pre-political in the sense that it did not occur readily to men that society could tolerate dissenting opinion within itself as a matter of course. The unity of society was upheld by the fiction that all its members thought the same" (1984, 19). In other words, one was either a part of society—within it, in which case one served the ruling classes in whatever ways one could—or one was marginalized. But such men as Raleigh, Bacon, Selden, and Donne—all of whom were variously central to and marginalized from the centers of power, and all of whom were friends of Jonson —were, by word and deed, at various times, alienated from the espoused values of the ruling classes.

As a (former) Roman Catholic, as a Horatian classicist, as a prober of the occult and the exotic, the unusual and the grotesque, Jonson had spent a lifetime defining a position for himself—and therefore for the artist—on the margins of courtly society. "As long as there is alienation," Jean Baudrillard has noted, "there is spectacle, action, scene" (1983, 130). It is not surprising, therefore, that, even after James's death, after his own paralytic stroke, after his quarrel with Inigo Jones and the execrable failure of his last plays, and after his contemptuous dismissal of the courtiers in his final ode to himself, Jonson continued to maintain a position of detachment from the merging of traditional folk culture and the emerging popular culture.

This position is evident in the reference to the Robin Hood legend in *The King's Entertainment at Welbeck*, which was presented for King Charles's visit to Bolsover Castle in 1633. The Castle was owned by Charles Cavendish, the Earl of Newcastle, who was Lord Warden of nearby Sherwood Forest. After surveying the local topography, a character named Accidence refers to a local folk custom of

> Lead-men . . .
> That turne round like grindlestones:
> . . . Which they dig out fro' the Delves,
> For their Bairnes-bread, Wines, and selves:
> Whom the Whetstone sharpes to eat,
> And cry, Milstones are good meat.
>
> (100–05)

One of these legendary figures can

> ... report you more odde tales
> Of our Outlaw *Robin-Hood*,
> That revell'd here in *Sherwood*;
> (Though he ne're shot in his Bow)
> Then au' men, or beleeve, or know.

(106–12)

The reference here to Robin Hood as "our Outlaw" blurs any distinction that might be made between folk culture and the culture of the court. Here we can see the Robin Hood legend in the process of being accommodated to the conventions by which and through which the values of this new culture were disseminated.

The Sad Shepherd is an especially significant example of how folk and courtly cultures resisted appropriation by the newly literate, and increasingly hegemonic, popular culture. In the play, conflicts between popular and courtly cultures and the ideological contradictions inherent in Stuart absolutism are everywhere apparent, and ambiguities are rampant. For example, before the play begins Jonson tries to manipulate his prospective audience's view of him by addressing them familiarly in the second person, but he deflects any resistence that might be directed back at him by speaking of himself in the third person:

> *He that hath feasted you these forty yeares,*
> *And fitted* Fables, *for your finer eares,*
> *Although at first, he scarce could hit the bore;*
> *Yet you, with patience harkning more and more,*
> *At length have growne up to him, and made knowne,*
> *The Working of his* Pen *is now your owne:*
> *He pray's you would vouchsafe, for your owne sake,*
> *To heare him this once more, but, sit awake.*

(ll. 1–8)

By presenting a version of himself as a disinterested observer of what he, at other times, tried so hard to make us believe were *his own* plays, Jonson, typically, tries to distance his "inner" or "true" self from anticipated criticism. This Horatian persona coaxes the audience into a hospitable frame of mind. The image of playwrighting as feasting, which anticipates the feast about which the play centers, recalls similar images of feasting and eating throughout Jonson's texts. And the self-deprecation of the fourth line and the patronizing flattery in the rest of that sentence likewise serve to remind us that we are re-meeting an old friend, the Horatian scholar-poet who stands at a remove and whose public face always hides his private self. For after the disarming admission that "*at first, he scarce could hit the bore,*" the passage turns, with the phrase "*Yet you,*" on us and tells us what we ought to do—namely, grow up to him, that is, learn to appreciate his art. The next line shifts the audience's attention away from the author, "*his* Pen," back to themselves —"*is now your own.*" Then another ploy is introduced; Jonson says he has now educated us—his audience—to a point where we, or at least those of us with "*finer eares,*" may assume his role of moral arbiter, but he asks—indeed pleads with us for our "*owne sake*"—to listen to him "*this once,*" and presumably final, time.

As usual, the emphasis on hearing and listening, rather than looking and seeing, undermines our preconceptions. And Jonson further highlights this distinction by portraying himself as a teacher and his audience as pupils. The passage moves from listening ("*eares*") to writing ("*his* Pen") and back to listening ("*heare*"). The audience, which "*at first*" was only capable of listening, has now become literate ("*now your owne*"). But what the passage gives with one hand it takes with the other; the reiteration of "*owne*" in the next line returns the audience once more to the status of listeners, but now they are in a changed state since they have "*growne up to*" him and can now assume his position and go about the task of educating others. Jonson thus accepts the literate members of his audience as peers, and this acceptance elevates the level of discourse from that of teacher-to-pupil to one between equals. This breaks down skepticism about accepting the unlikely cross-cultural hybrid: " . . . a Tale/*Of* Robin-hood's *inviting from the Vale*/ *Of* Be'voir, *all the* Shep'ards *to a Feast*" (ll. 15–17). Here, the word *"Feast"* at the end of the line and the end of the sentence draws attention and recalls the earlier *"feast"* that Jonson reminds his audience he has provided them for four decades (a clear indication that the play was not begun sometime earlier and abandoned). In a reversal of the conventional roles of host/parasite and patron/poet, Jonson portrays himself as a kind of Dionysian "big man" or great provider, a host/patron to those in need of sustenance. This feasting metaphor, so integral to Jonson's aesthetic, foregrounds the poet's role as transmitter of moral values.

The feast is but the most obvious means of drawing attention to the drama as *mimesis*, not just in the conventional sense as a representation of reality, but also in the sense of evoking sympathetic participation in the performance of a narrator such as Plato described in *The Republic* (393–94).[11] Plato's goes on to suggest that there are two kinds of *mimesis*, one good and one bad. Good *mimesis* is that which calls attention to itself, and bad *mimesis* is that which attempts to "fool" the observer or listener into believing that he or she is witnessing "reality" or the "truth." Plato identifies this latter kind of *mimesis* with witchcraft (602d). Jonson, I want to claim, practices the "good" kind of *mimesis*, and this is what distinguishes him from other English Renaissance writers.

I base this claim on several observations. First, I believe that in the Renaissance the sonnet sequence was a chief means of defining an authorial persona, a self that would give the illusion of speaking in a text as in "real" life, an illusion of "voice," of full presence. And I think it is significant that, unlike Spenser, Sidney, Shakespeare, and many others, Jonson did not write a sonnet sequence. Indeed, he scarcely wrote any sonnets *at all*, and in his conversations with Drummond he cursed Petrarch for redacting verses into sonnets (ll. 60–63). Thus, in contra-distinction to those who fashioned a self in a sonnet sequence and then went on to write other texts in which that self was an unacknowledged narrative presence, Jonson's texts—both nondramatic and dramatic—are full of (failed) attempts to define a self that is always in progress, always shifting, always rambling, never fixed, never satisfied with itself, never finished.

In his fascinating study *Shakespeare's Perjured Eye*, Joel Fineman contends that "in his sonnets Shakespeare invents a genuinely new poetic subjectivity," but Fineman's argument that "that this poetic subjectivity . . . extends by disrupting what until Shakespeare's sonnets is the normative nature of poetic person and poetic persona" (1985, 1) might be supplemented in light of Jonson's Horatian persona.[12] The nature of this supplement is to suggest that the Shakespearean persona tends to make the subject "see" itself as what Husserl, following Kant, called a transcendental ego. Such a subject, as Antony Easthope has explained, sees itself as an *absolutely* free agent, centre and origin of action, unproduced, given once and for all; in the words of Shakespeare's Coriolanus

> As if a man were author of himself
> And knew no other kin.
>
> (5.3.36–37)

But in contrast to this absolute subject position that "is produced in discourse so as to deny that it is produced at all, to 'see' itself only as a transcendental ego," there is "a relative position" that *is* "produced with some degree of recognition that it *is* so produced" (Easthope 1983, 28).

What I want to suggest is that Shakespeare's persona suggests that it "sees" itself—and is "seen" to the extent that it is "seen" at all—as a transcendental ego, whereas Jonson's Horatian persona *continually* reminds itself and us that it is in the process of producing itself and we are also in the process of producing it. Shakespeare writes about himself as a self *only* in his sonnets, and even there it is quite a transcendental self. Jonson, on the other hand, *continually* writes about himself; he *repeatedly* and *insistently* calls attention to himself, even when he "pretends" to be writing about others—his friends, his children, etc. He lards his plays with prologues and prefaces, with notes and observations, and repeatedly inserts a version of himself into his plays.

The effect of all of these efforts at self-fashioning—and they are all obviously *failed* efforts—is to remind us continually of his insecurity, of his neediness, of his *lack* of a secure selfhood. Shakespeare *never* inserts himself into his plays. And this has the effect of making us see him as an absolute transcendental ego, as a masterful consummate artist both of himself and of his plays. (The debate over whether or not Prospero is a version of Shakespeare's self is the exception that proves the rule here, for *if* he is a version of the author, he is a consummately transcendental ego.) Jonson is always busy making himself known; he is forever seen as a careerist, whereas Shakespeare is *never* seen in this way.

In a Shakespearean play, the absence of a narrator challenges the audience to produce meaning, to suspend disbelief and accept the scenes, characters, and language as real; in a Jonsonian play the narrator, as represented speaker, is given priority, and we are invited to accept this speaker as the authentic voice of the author. This has the effect of constantly calling our attention to the fact that we are watching—or reading—a play. As Easthope has pointed out, the Shakespearean model encourages us to "run together the poet as historical author and the poet as implied speaker," or, in a more sophisticated version of the same thing, to see the implied speaker as other than the author, yet to see the author as responsible for the speaker as an "adopted *persona,* a mask which itself becomes his expression" (Easthope 1982, 140).

The prologue to *The Sad Shepherd* focuses attention on the author and calls attention to the fact that what we are about to see or read is a *mimesis*—an *imitation* (or representation) of "reality." But these efforts to convince us that the play is under authorial control only serve to put us on guard and invite us to resist the author's view of "his own" work. It seems axiomatic that the more a text claims to be the property of a speaker represented in it, the more it draws attention to the fact that it most certainly is not, that there is no way to enforce such a proprietory right. While an author's attention to the details of publication was born out of the anxiety over retaining benefits derived from producing a text, the anxiety concerning the *loss* of control was symptomatic of an awareness that control was always already problematic.

No matter how much an author attempts to control the dissemination of his or her texts, no matter how much an author seeks to guide and direct interpretation, in the end, the audience—collectively and individually—interprets those texts in accordance with their perceptions and their own interests. His awareness of this fact may have galled and/or delighted Jonson. Judging from documentary records, his reactions appear to have been mixed, but whether or not it was part of his intention to leave us with that or any other impression is only relevant insofar as we recognize that that intention is produced by and is part of our reading of those texts that make up Jonson's *oeuvre*.

3

The Persistence of Pagan Pastimes:
Difference in the Organic Community

If ever GORGON were seene in the shape of
a woman, hee hath seene her in my description—
Epicoene (3.7.21–22)

I n the second chapter of his study of the English pastoral tradition, *The Country and the City*, Raymond
Williams remembers a sentence from F. R. Leavis and
Denys Thompson's *Culture and Environment* (1933): "The
'organic community' of 'Old England' had disappeared,"
and noted that "the change is very recent indeed." This
view, Williams noted, "was primarily based on the books
of George Sturt, which appeared between 1907 and 1923"
(1973, 9). And he went on to observe that the decline of
the social values associated with an agrarian society—stability, orderliness, neighborliness, and slow cyclic change
—has always been located in the recent past. Williams, I
want to emphasize, was critical but by no means contemptuous or dismissive of the values of the "organic community." As he went on to point out, "Nostalgia ... is universal and persistent; only other men's nostalgias offend."
Here Williams anticipated one of the main premises of

poststructuralism: that there is no escape from logocentrism, from the metaphysics of presence that privileges speech over writing. Williams's humility enabled him to have this important insight. He was never so arrogant as to believe that he, or anyone else, individually or collectively, could decide what "History" was all about, nor did he presume to identify his brand of Marxism with objective scientific "Truth." Instead he worked with the assumption that the past means "different things at different times, and quite different values are [constantly] being brought into question." The things facts tell us, he noted, "are not all of the same mode." We make "structures of feeling" from these facts, and, he held, "We can only analyze these important structures . . . if we make, from the beginning, these critical discriminations" (1973, 12).

In the spirit of Williams's critique of culture, which always includes self-critique, I want to reinvoke Jonson's presence at the inception of popular culture. I want to do this by recalling how, in his pathbreaking book *Drama and Society in the Age of Jonson*, L. C. Knights argued that while Jonson was a classicist, his art was "intimately related to the popular tradition of individual and social morality" (1937, 151). Knights went on to praise Jonson for being "one of the main channels of communication with an almost vanished [folk] tradition" and for his "anti-acquisitive attitude expressed as bare moral statement" (191).

In a thoughtful reevaluation of Knights's book, Don E. Wayne has pointed out that *Bartholomew Fair* is "the only major play of Jonson's omitted from Knights's discussion." This, Wayne argues, is significant because in that play Jonson not only satirizes popular taste but identifies his own interests with those tastes: "the logic of the comic resolution in *Bartholomew Fair* conveys a sense of authorial self-irony that is lacking in the earlier plays" (1984, 121). *Bartholomew Fair*, Wayne asserts, "is the model of a new ideology" (122) in which "the traditional dichotomy between [Apollonian] reason and the [Dionysian] passions was . . . attenuated by the introduction of

... the 'countervailing passion' of *interest*." And this, Wayne holds, led to "the emergence of another modern phenomenon, the problem of alienation" (123). Since patriarchy "was the common basis of argumentation in conflicting doctrines concerning the foundations of state and society ... it is not surprising to find Jonson employing the image of 'home' in such different contexts as 'To Penshurst,' ... and at the end of *Bartholomew Fair*" (126). Therefore, Wayne concludes, if we, unlike Knights, distinguish between aristocratic and middle-class views of patriarchy, we can avoid replicating "the nostalgia and the longing that we find, at times, in Jonson's own works." For, "where Knights shares Jonson's nostalgia, he lacks the seventeenth century poet's capacity for self-irony" (127).

Wayne's corrective for nostalgia turns out to be none other than the shibboleth of high modernism, self-ironization. But this voice is by no means free of a very special kind of longing for a lost patriarchal security. When Wayne says that Jonson "provided his audiences with a model for the society which they themselves were already in the process of creating" (129), this is self-ironization with a vengeance. Wayne here praises Jonson for revitalizing a faltering patriarchy and for helping to construct the nuclear family as a *new* patriarchal ideal. What could be more nostalgic?

Terry Eagleton is caught in a similar decidedly nondialectical contradiction when he notes that

> The reports of educational bodies and official inquiries into the teaching of English ... are strewn with nostalgic back-references to the 'organic' community of Elizabethan England in which nobles and groundlings found a common meeting-place in the Shakespearian theatre, and which might still be reinvented today. (1983, 28)

He too is speaking in the self-ironized voice of high modernism. "Organic societies," Eagleton goes on to say, "are just convenient myths for belabouring the mechanized life of modern industrial capitalism" (36).

My question is: if that is all they are—convenient myths

—why do they keep appearing in the texts of those for whom their allure is supposedly demystified? William Empson, one of Eagleton's heroes, dealt with this matter most effectively. In *Some Versions of Pastoral*, he noted that

> in pastoral you take a limited life and pretend it is the full and normal one, and a suggestion that one must do this with all life, because the normal is itself limited, is easily put into the trick though not necessary to its power. Conversely any expression of the idea that all life is limited may be regarded as only a trick of pastoral, perhaps chiefly intended to hold our attention and sympathy for some limited life, though again this is not necessary to it either on grounds of truth or beauty .... (1960, 111–12)

To explore this matter further, we might look again at T. S. Eliot's excoriation of modern life as wasted and hollow and his harkening back to the lost organic community of (pre-)Elizabethan England. As I have noted, Jonson played a key role in Eliot's effort to construct a vision of the intellectual/artist who could rewrite the drama of that community's fall. In his essay on Jonson, he argued that "not many people are capable of discovering for themselves the beauty which is only to be found after labour." Accordingly, he said, intellectuals had to be taught how to understand Jonson, but that was not to be done by teaching Jonson's classical sources or the social mannerisms of his time. Those things had to be picked up from the air one breathed—that is, they had to be part of one's heritage, one's family, or, to put it more accurately, those elements had to be *assumed* to be part of the aristocratic heritage that lower-middle-class intellectuals were taught to serve. To enter the organic community, one had to saturate oneself in Jonson's work "as a whole," for "in order to enjoy him at all, we must get to the center of his work and his temperament, and that we must see him unbiased by time, as a contemporary." It was useless to try to encourage ordinary people to pretend they were living in seventeenth century London. So

Eliot encouraged intellectuals to see Jonson "as a contemporary" and set him "in our London" (1986a, 106).

With the onset of World War II, Eliot had to relocate the utopian promise of the organic community in the collective unconscious. But the idea of a lost organic community continued to inform assessments of Jonson's plays and poems. In the same chapter in *The Country and the City* in which Williams called Leavis and Thompson's use of the phrase "organic community" into question, Williams attempted to make literal the utopian vision outlined in "To Penshurst." He warned that "we can make no simple extension from Penshurst to a whole country civilization. The forces of pride, greed and calculation are evidently active among landowners as well as among city merchants and courtiers." But the word "evidently" here betrays a certain lack of confidence on Williams's part. And the next sentence shows even greater self-doubt: "What is being celebrated," Williams writes, "is then perhaps an idea of rural society, as against the pressures of a new age" (1973, 28).

In the end Williams asserts that Jonson's pastoral has no material social base whatsoever. It could be no more than "perhaps an idea" because "the social order is seen as part of a wider order: what is now sometimes called a natural order, with metaphysical sanctions"; for Williams this is clearly a fantasy, "a mystification" in which "the provident land is seen as Eden . . . . Except that it is not seen as Paradise; it is seen as Penshurst, a natural order that is arranged by a proprietary lord and lady." And since there are no laborers in the poem, no one who does the actual work of preserving the garden estate, Williams concludes that "To call this a natural order is then an abuse of language" (29, 31, 33).[1]

Williams bases his reading on the assumption that Jonson looked upon the community celebrated in "To Penshurst" as "natural." But the poem does not say, nor does it even imply, that Penshurst is such a community. Quite the contrary, the poem creates a fantasy world located somewhere between myth and imagination, a world of dryads, satyrs, and fauns, which enables us to see—just as we see through a disguise—how art differs from, and in many respects stands "above," while at the same time it is dependent upon, nature.

In this respect the poem does just what Williams attacks it for *not* doing. Through a metonymic view of the Sidney estate, it articulates a utopian ideal; it does not present a "realistic" portrait of life on a seventeenth century country estate. Thus, while on one level the poem appears to idealize feudal social relationships, on another level it undermines the goals and aspirations of both the declining aristocracy and the rising bourgeoisie. It tells those with newly acquired wealth that they cannot bring back the chivalric glory of the past. And the poem simultaneously tells those who wish to hang on to hereditary privilege that their way of life is anachronistic.

If we insist on reading the poem as a monovocal declaration of a single transcendental authorial intention, we must blind ourselves to this indeterminancy; we cannot entertain such heteroglossia, such polysemy, as possible supplementary "meanings" or readings. Even historically informed readings of the poem may fail to take such possibilities into account if they are restricted to fitting the poem into an "ideological" paradigm. For example, in his book-length study of the poem, Wayne maintains that it is "clearly intended as an ideological statement." We are not told exactly how Wayne can be so sure of Jonson's intentions—or why Jonson would have had such an intention—but Wayne asserts confidently that the poem is "the result . . . of a project that simultaneously asserts an ideology and places it in question." In support of this assertion, Wayne postulates that Jonson had "a complex strategy for rationalization" and that what he rationalized was his "intuitive grasp of a contradiction in his poem's ideological purpose" (1984, 20).

But we do not need to construct such complex motives and attribute them to Jonson unless we wish to reinvest in a humanist idealization of patriarchy. With this motive demystified, there is *no need* to hypothesize that Jonson intuitively grasps anything. It is enough to see Wayne's informed effort to understand how "To Penshurst" encapsulates emergent capitalism's appropriation of the ideology of feudalism and the constructed tradition folk culture upon which it was based, and realize that this explodes the conventional critical attribution to Jonson of a monovocal intention to glorify feudal hierarchies. Wayne effectively closes the tradition of intentionality and clears the way for more theoretically sophisticated readings. After reading Wayne on Jonson, we can drop the fiction that if we could but determine Jonson's purpose in writing the poem we could settle any question of the poem's meaning once and for all.

We might begin with an effort to defamiliarize this very familiar poem. For example, we might notice that the first of many strange things about "To Penshurst" is that it is written as though it were spoken to a house. We are merely eavesdroppers—merely allowed, as it were, almost by accident, to listen in as the speaker addresses the estate. So right away, we are asked—and in some ways *required*—to accept what we know to be a fiction, and the act of accepting this fiction, of allowing ourselves to believe it, is a key to reading—a key to how we are *required* to read—the poem. A second curious thing about the poem—the more closely we read the poem the more curious it becomes—is that the speaker does not describe how the house looks, how it appears, but instead tells us how it does not look.[2]

These two fictions—deliberate ruptures in the *mimesis* of the normative reading process, whereby a speaker describes or represents to us a scene he or she has witnessed —encourage us to suspend our disbelief. They put us in a state of receptivity, of willingness to accept a fictitious description of a country estate as "reality." But this description is delayed. From the description of what Penshurst *does not* look like, we do *not* move to an anticipated comparative description of its actual appearance. Instead we move to the Dionysian Mount where "the *Dryads* doe resort,/ Where PAN, and BACCHUS their high feasts have made" (ll. 10–11). Now we see the purpose of the opening. By initially calling upon us to suspend our disbelief, the poet has made us willing to accept this fantastic description. Because we have been prepared by the double negative fictions of indirect discourse and non-description, we accept this description; we accept this fantastic world much as we accept the mimetic "reality" of the primitive in Jonson's antimasques. With our minds cast back to this childlike state of receptivity, of preconsciousness, we regain—or at least we allow ourselves to *imagine* that we do—a primal state of oneness, of participatory consciousness where we see everything as alive and interrelated and where we know the world through direct apprehension.

By the time we arrive at the Dionysian Mount, we have been prepared by the double negative introduction to accept a reality we know to be false in terms of rational discourse, but which we are prepared to accept as true once our minds have been reawakened to this childlike state of consciousness. The speaker is, in this sense, constituted as a magician who rejects rational discourse and "realistic" description and representation. His discourse breaks down—or at least blurs—the boundaries between mind and body, subject and object, conscious and unconscious, humans and nature. By beginning with what might be seen as an oversight of the Penshurst estate from the vantage point of the Dionysian Mount, the speaker *returns* us, so to speak, to a point in the past that is not necessarily a historical point—not, that is, an actual discernible, documentable point but a point *beyond* (i.e., behind) history. This prehistorical mythical point is also, ontogenically, an equally nonverifiable point beyond/behind the history of consciousness, the trace of which may be glimpsed in ancient written and pictorial accounts (vase and cave paintings) of Dionysian rituals such as the "high feasts" alluded to in the poem (l. 11).

Instead of re-presenting the appearance of a veiled reality, this speaker establishes his discourse in such a way as to ask us to believe that he is presenting life completely and immediately. He constitutes himself in such a way as to suggest that we should accept his vision as an apocalyptical tearing away of the veil of appearance. And, true to the apocalyptic—as opposed to prophetic—consciousness, his mode is the written—as opposed to the spoken —word: "all the *Muses* met" (l. 14) under the tree planted at the birth of the, as yet, unnamed poet (Sidney), in whose bark "are cut the names/ Of many a SYLVANE" (ll. 15–16). The poet is thus one who *writes*, as opposed to one who "merely" *speaks*. And here, on the Dionysian Mount, where "the ruddy *Satyres* oft provoke/ The lighter *faunes*" (ll. 17–18), we arrive at the central image of fertility, "the *Ladies oke*" (l. 18). We have been prepared for this feminized phallic image by the evocation of the rites that took place "Beneath the broad beech, and the chestnut shade" (l. 12)—that is, away from the city and the house itself, which stands for the civil world of men, and these rites also took place out of sight of the masculine (Apollonian) sun. This is a fecund feminine world named for Barbara Gamage (l. 19), who gave birth to 12 children, but in the poem all images of femininity, fertility, and birth are distinctly separate from—outside—the country house itself, where we assume these children were born. And while we move from the periphery to the center of the house as we read the poem, neither the exterior nor the interior of the house is described in any detail.

Instead, the poem suddenly moves from the fertile forested scene to "The lower land" (l. 22) of domesticated animals and civil order, a restricted Apollonian world where we are asked to believe that "The painted partrich ... / ... is willing to be kill'd" (ll. 29–30), and fish "runne into thy net" (l. 33). And, of course, we *do* believe this because we have been prepared to believe it, but we do so at the cost of our own credibility. In other words, the poem resists our entry into the world it describes; it *almost* disallows *mimesis*. It is *very difficult* not to suspend our disbelief when we read it. By presenting outlandish events and incidents as though they were matter-of-fact everyday occurrences, the poem challenges us *not* to believe what we are told. But, in accordance with the utopian folk tradition upon which it is drawn—epitomized by the early fourteenth century ballad *The Land of Cokaygne*—the hyperbole undermines the reader's ability to accept the reality of the very thing the poem pretends to re-present, the obeisance of nature to the country estate that personifies the men who own it and who seek to control everything and everyone within and around it.

The poem, then, doth affirm too much. It puts into discourse things that—in a perfectly ordered "organic community"—would be tacitly assumed, part of the very air that is breathed. But here, through the shift from the Dionysian to the Apollonian—which requires us to believe that birds, fish, and indeed all nature willingly sacrifice themselves to "his Lordships" (l. 64) house—the poem subverts the sincerity of the speaker's praise. Because of its effusiveness, its all too obvious exaggeration if not downright inversion of the idea that humans *should* serve nature, the poem constantly threatens to become a distorted denial, a parody, of the social hierarchy it officially affirms. Therefore, it allows us to glimpse what is just below the surface of consciousness and also below the surface of officialdom: the repressed and sublimated urges and impulses suggested by the feasts that are alluded to in the past tense but forsaken when the poem abruptly descends to the lower land of civil society. And since we know that even in an ideal society, a utopia, birds and fish would not *willingly* be killed, we doubt that "every child" (l. 44) may reach the fruit that grows in Penshurst's walled gardens. Similarly, when we are told that those walls "are rear'd with no mans ruine, no mans grone" (ll. 45–46) we suspect that this is also untrue, even if we did not know or suspect it previously. And when we read that "There's none, that dwell about them, wish them downe" (l. 47), we are startled by the suggestion that anyone *could* wish them down.

Thus the poem increasingly and progressively undermines the premises it ostensibly seeks to affirm. Its denials, like its affirmations, subvert themselves. We are repeatedly told things that we have no need to be told—or at least that we *would* have no need to be told if these very things were not at issue. So by the time we get to the scene describing the peasant's presentation of gifts to the lord and lady of the manor, our credulity is strained beyond the breaking point, and when we are told that the gift of cheese is equivalent ("or else" [l. 53]) to "their ripe daughters" (l. 54) we smile because, if we have paid attention, we suspect—although we cannot be sure—that the discourse has become parodic of the reality it pretends to affirm. We suspect this because we have been led to doubt the sincerity of the hyperbolic speaker, and also because the analogy between the ripeness of the peasant's daughters and the cheeses mocks—even as it supports—the idea that women are but fruitful commodities, which, we are told in the next lines of the poem, are unneeded anyway.

The description of the lordship's communal feast that follows, when read in light of the "high feasts" of Pan and Bacchus, which took place outdoors "Beneath the broad beech, and the chest-nut shade" (l. 12), is similarly problematized. These high feasts defied the rules of (patriarchal) society—which required that a sacrificial domestic animal be properly slaughtered (by men) and cooked (by women) before being served and eaten indoors. Instead, these feasts centered upon the rebellious acts of a band of women who left their homes and roamed the forested mountains where they chased wild animals, dismembered them with their bare hands (*sparagmos*), and ate them raw (*omophagia*), thus destroying the boudaries between human and animal, male and female.[3]

Moreover, the speaker's bravado indicates that he is uncomfortable at the feast. He lets us know that he knows he does not fit in and tells us that he is only allowed to be there at the discretion of his lordship. He has no *legitimate* right to sit and eat "thy lords owne meate" (l. 62). The fact that Jonson told Drummond he was invited to dine with Lord Salisbury but "he had none of his meate" (*Conv.* 320) underscores the importance of the fact that the speaker in "To Penshurst" is "not faine to sit (as some, this day,/ At great mens tables) and yet dine away" (ll. 65–66). Thus while this self-professed glutton is pleased that "he shall finde plentie of meate" (l. 70) at his lordship's table, and even goes so far as to dream of being owner and master of the estate (l. 74), he, unlike the royal huntsman and his son, is clearly an outsider. Indeed, the poem may be read as an attempted appropriation by the speaker —a representative of the new class of professional writers—of the tradition of primogeniture and courtly poetry that the estate represents and which the Sidney family epitomized. The speaker inherits the estate by memorializing its significance, its meaning as a mark of a receding past, in a poem. This is a way of passing it on to his "sons." And in some ways, the poem suggests—or hopes—this is a better way since the poem embodies the spiritual essence of the estate, as opposed to its mere physical presence, its literality, which the nouveau riche merchants and entrepreneurs' estates cannot. Such new estates are ostentatiously massive, but they are not monumental.

When the king and his son visit Penshurst, it is, significantly, the "good lady" (l. 84), not the lord, on whom they heap their praise and who reaps "The just reward of her high huswifery" (l. 85). But even here the speaker does not seem able to offer unambivalent praise. The next lines read that "To have her linnen, plate, and all things nigh,/ When shee was farre" (ll. 86–87). Here, even if we supply the absent subject and verb, i.e., "She desired to have . . . "—that is, even if we supply the pointedly absent *desire*—we are still left with the contradiction of how the lady can have all her housewifely things near her "When she is farre," and we are also left to wonder where she goes and why. In the new middle-class nuclear family, a woman's place is in the home.

But at Penshurst, we are told, perhaps a bit too insistently, that "Thy lady's noble, fruitfull, chaste withall" (l. 90). Here again the assertion calls attention to—and thus puts in question—something that we might have taken for granted. For the question of the lady's fruitfullness and chastity might not occur to us if the poem had not prepared us to ask it by its hyperbolic praise. And when this is followed by the statement that "His children the great lord may call his owne" (l. 91), we are led to ask why we *need* to be told this. Is it a matter of doubt? Is there some reason why he should not believe they are his own? And, having raised these questions, we may be led to ask why are they called "A fortune, in this age, but rarely knowne"? (l. 92) Why are they "rarely knowne"? The line suggests that some aristocratic women had resisted having a child every year—or, alternately, that some aristocratic men, patriarchs—feared that their patrimony was running out, that their sexual potency was waning, that their class privilege was dwindling.

The qualifying phrase "in this age" reminds us of a sense of loss; it signifies a longing to capture a fleeting and receding—and perhaps fantasized—time of wholeness and harmony, when children were "at one" with their parents and their cultural as well as physical environment. But now we must imagine in what sense these children should be "knowne." The poem, again, seems to be trying to raise, in some oblique fashion, a question as to their paternity, their legitimacy. And just after these questions are raised in our minds, we are told that "They . . . have beene taught religion" (l. 93), a statement that, again, belies its own surface meaning when we consider the context and question why the children need to be "*taught* religion." The phrase itself is oyxmoronic. Surely things have come to a desperate pass when children of noblemen need to be *taught* religion, when the beliefs and values that they should spontaneously absorb from merely growing up in a culture have to be learned in the way academic subjects are. What greater testimony to their alienation from what should be their own ethos do we need than that their "gentler spirits" also have to be "Taught to pray" (ll. 94–95)? And, finally, what are we to make of the fact that their parents' habits are so alien to them that they must "Reade, in their vertuous parents noble parts,/ The mysteries of manners, armes, and arts" (ll. 97–98)? For as Juliet Flower MacCannell has pointed out, "Bakhtin has taught us [that] once a value has to be voiced, it is no longer truly a value, but only a symbol of it, a topic of discourse, and it ceases to organize life" (1983, 912).

My reading of "To Penshurst" sees the poem as constantly and consistently undermining any spontaneous acceptance of the ethos of the class the poem has usually been thought to celebrate. This reading may be perverse, but it can be meticulously documented. The speaker in "To Penshurst," like Edgar at the end of *King Lear*, repeatedly tells us that "we that are young/ Shall never see so much, nor live so long" (5.2.327–28), shall never recapture the animistic, i.e., mythic, consciousness and communal harmony of those who have gone before us. The poem looks back to a time of logocentric wholeness and harmony, a time *before* consciousness was severed from knowledge, before awareness of *mimesis*, before separation from the mother and the mother tongue, before the fall into the symbolic order represented by and through writing.

As Empson saw, the pastoral mode was a means by which and through which the aristocratic, courtly ideology was articulated, just as the prophetic tradition had been a vehicle for the dissemination of Protestant imperialism since the time of John Bale and John Foxe. And, like "To Penshurst," *The Sad Shepherd* undermines both of these associations by mixing pastoral with folk traditions. Indeed, as David Wiles has noted, "The educated classes, from the time of Langland onwards, had little sympathy for popular manifestations of the Robin Hood cult" (1981, 53). Thus the omission of any reference to Robin Hood's specious aristocratic background in the play preserves the traditional identification of the legendary outlaw with the culture of the lower classes, especially the rural agrarian peasantry. The play is marked by such exclusions, as when, for example, the speaker of the prologue asserts that he wishes to dispel

> ... *an Heresie of late let fall;*
> *That Mirth by no meanes fits a* Pastorall.
>
> (ll. 29–30)

This may refer to a specific work; perhaps *The Shepherd's Holyday*, Joseph Rutter's parody of Thomas Dekker's immensely popular celebration of middle-class life, *The Shoemaker's Holiday*. Rutter's play had been acted at Whitehall, and Jonson wrote a prefatory poem of extremely faint praise when it was published in January 1635. This pastoral play blends Arcadian and courtly elements in a story concerning Thirsis's grief for the loss of his Sylvia, whom he supposes was carried off by satyr, and the death—by magic—of the huntress Nernia who is in love with poor Hylas but who is courted by wealthy Daphnis. After many sad scenes, all are reunited in a joyful reaffirmation of the hierarchical and patriarchal values of the court.

Of course *The Sad Shepherd* was not necessarily written in response to any one play. In the 1630s pastoral, a prime vehicle for the articulation of the ethos of the court, became "almost uniformly humourless" (Barton 1984, 342) because it was losing what Louis Montrose, following Empson, has described as its ability to "mediate class differences and ideological contradictions, so as to make a particular version of 'the social order' possible" (1983, 417). After the passage of the Petition of Right in 1629, the year Charles dissolved Parliament, the hierarchical distinctions—which were more than merely symbolic boundaries—upon which the social order was predicated rapidly deteriorated. As a result, the mystifications of class that pastoralism both reflected and promoted were exposed, and that mode of expression continued to be placed before the public. Phineas Fletcher's *Sicelides*, written in 1614, was printed in 1631; John Fletcher's *Faithful Shepherdess*, written in 1609, was revived in 1634; Thomas Randolph's *Amyntas* was written sometime between 1632 and 1635, and Ralph Knevet's *Rhodon and Iris* (1631) and Walter Montague's *Shepherd's Paradise* (1633) were popular with upper-class audiences who were encouraged to look back to the Golden Age of Elizabeth as an oblique utopia.

The Sad Shepherd parodies that sentimental retrospective. In its obliquely Dionysian world, as in Rabelais's depiction of the medieval carnival, conventional hierarchies are turned upside down. Michael Drayton had caught something of this in his account of the Robin Hood legend in the twenty-sixth song of *Poly-Olbion*, where it is not Robin Hood but the Diana-figure, Maid Marian, who hunts and kills the deer (ll. 352–58). In *The Sad Shepherd* not only does Maid Marian hunt, kill, and dress the deer, but other masculine figures such as Friar Tuck, George a Greene, and Much the Miller's son stay behind to "see the Bower drest;/ And fit the fine devises for the Feast" (1.3.3–4).

Unobtrusively they go about the task of shaping the natural world to their simple needs. They celebrate nature, and even alter it in moderate ways, but they are careful not to despoil it. Friar Tuck, the prelate of this grove, tells George he must take "care to make the Baldrick trim,/ And Garland that must crowne, or her, or him,/ Whose Flock this yeare, hath brought the earliest Lambe" (1.3.5–7). And George responds that he will "cut the Table out o'the green sword/ . . . / To carve the Guests large seats; and these laid in/ With turfe (as soft and smooth as the Moles skin)" (1.3.9–12). Here "a faire Dyall" (1.3.15) reminds these social outcasts of passing time, but at the same time it softens and meliorates that reminder. Everything is done to emphasize the ritualistic aspect of the occasion, its separation from ordinary life outside the forest. This also serves to remind us of the fragility of this world, its vergence on extinction. When we are told that Robin Hood's entertainments "must have all the rites" (1.3.17), we see those rites in relationship to the quasi-Dionysian rites Jonson had provided for James and Charles, the efficacy of which became increasingly more problematic as Puritans in Parliament demanded restraint and took control of the government.

This impulse to preserve a world teetering on the brink of disaster may be traced back to the convergence of the medieval world of carnival and the Renaissance world of courtly pastoral. Around 1283 the French troubadour Adam de la Halle had written a *pastourelle* entitled *Jeu de Robin et Marion* that became absorbed into the May Games; local people began choosing a young woman and a young man to preside over their celebration as Maid Marian and Robin Hood (D&T 42n1).[4] In the fourteenth century John Gower adapted de la Halle's *pastourelle* for a courtly audience in his *Speculum Meditantis* (1376–79), and during the next century Robin Hood games and pastoral plays evolved side by side but independently of one another. By the sixteenth century, two distinct genres, played before two separate audiences, developed: the one local and popular, the other urban and courtly.

In *The Sad Shepherd*, as in de la Halle's *pastourelle*, a feast provides an escape from routine existence and allows people to liberate themselves from a culture consecrated by social hierarchies. Jonson appropriated the figure of Dame Douce from another of de la Halle's *pastourelles*, *Jeu de la Feuillee*, where a prostitute named Dame Douce speaks for popular rebellion. Here Douce is protected by fairies who represent the world of license and revelry, a world that rules with impunity on May Day Eve, much as Oberon and Titania do in *A Midsummer Night's Dream*. That play was still being performed in private theaters for a courtly audience in the 1630s

(Butler 1984, 131), and there, as in *The Sad Shepherd* and de la Halle's *pastourelles*, women rebel against patriarchal authority through an expression of sexual choice within the context of festivity. In his study of Rabelais and his world, Bakhtin explains how such repressed Dionysianism results in "the suspension of the Church's exclusive power [which] brings back the uncrowned pagan gods," but the carnivalesque is not exclusively retrospective, not necessarily nostalgic, for "The feast looks into the future, and this future acquires not only a utopian character but also the primitive archaic form of prophecies, curses, and blessings" (1984, 260). What Bakhtin did not emphasize is that, as in the ancient legends of the maenads, sexually rebellious women dominate that animistic world.

In *The Sad Shepherd* the supposed drowning of the shepherdess Earine prompts Aeglamour (aeger = sick, lámour = lover), to express desire to return to a chaotic presocial state. He curses "those rich Shepherds, dwelling in this Vale" (1.3.55) for Earine's loss and dreams of making the river Trent

> . . . drowne their Herds, their cattle, and their corne,
> Break downe their Mils, their Dams, ore-turne their
>   weeres,
> And see their houses, and whole lively-hood
> Wrought into water . . . .

(1.3.59–62)

This destructive aspect of water is juxtaposed with a positive aspect of renewal, the alternative world of Robin Hood's bower. As Bakhtin says of the folly of the May Day feast, this world represents "the opposite of wisdom . . . . the other side, the lower stratum" (1984, 260), but it also has the potential of liberating people from routine labor and from the strictures organized religion imposed upon physical pleasure. Aeglamour's rejection of the existing world places him in alliance with the medieval Christian view that one should renounce worldly distractions and concentrate on spiritual salvation, but it also implies the rejection of the parsimonious sobriety, orderliness, and rationality that the discourse of the new middle classes valorized.

Robin Hood and his band are outlaws in the most literal sense of the word; i.e, there must be a lawful world from which they are excluded. They live apart from, but in juxtaposition to, the social and cultural mainstream that, in the 1630s, was becoming increasingly middle class and puritanical. The "sourer sort/ Of Shepherds," Clarion explains, denigrate singing and dancing. Friar Tuck wishes these killjoys

> ... were not hurried more
> With Covetise and Rage, when to their store
> They adde the poore mans Eaneling, and dare sell
> Both Fleece, and Carkasse, not gi'ing him the Fell.
> (1.4.22–25)

Such protests against the business world's takeover of an older agrarian economy punctuate the play. At the time it was written, what was known as the Sabbatarian Controversy had become a focal point of dissent between pious, industrious inhabitants of the cities and large towns who attended local grammar schools and tended their business, and those—still the vast majority—who "were not unduly troubled about salvation, who were content with their horizons of knowledge and experience, and whose daily or seasonal routine required no mastery of print or script" (Cressy 1980, 1–2).[5]

Social historians have encouraged us to see this latter group, in contradistinction to middle-class Puritans, as wanting to preserve a less restrictive, more closely knit, rural, agrarian society where people lived in small communities. On weekends, instead of—or in addition to—attending church and listening to sermons, these people participated in such ritualistic exercises as May Games, morris dances, and informal sports, carnivalesque pastimes closely related to the "old religion," Roman Catholicism, and to theatricality. As has been noted, during the last decades of the sixteenth century, Gossen and

Munday had attacked the theater as an immoral institution. In 1583 Philip Stubbes had published his infla-
matory *Anatomy of Abuses*, and in 1599 Dr. John Rai-
nolds followed with *Th' Overthrow of Stage Plays*. The
next year saw the publication of William Vaughan's *Golden Grove*, which argued vehemently that plays should
not be allowed in a Christian country. A second edition
was issued eight years later. During the next quarter of
a century the attacks subsided. But in 1633 William
Prynne revived the assault with his encyclopedic *His-
trio Mastix, the Players Scourge, or Actors Tragaedie*, in
which he quoted Jonson's *Bartholomew Fair* as evidence
of the sin of transvestism (H&S 10.213–14). In addition
to plays, Prynne singles out "May-games, amorous Pastor-
alls, lascivious effeminate Musicke, excessive laughter,
luxurious disorderly Christmas-keeping, [and] Mummeries" as "unchristian pastimes" (quoted in Barish 1981,
85).[6]

Implicit in such attacks is a paranoid fear of blurring
gender distinctions, a theme glanced at in *Volpone* and *The
Alchemist* and explored at length in *Epicoene*. The puppet show scene near the end of *Bartholomew Fair* is emblematic of this masculine hysteria at the prospect of any
movement toward the feminine, a hysteria King James
himself evidenced in 1620 when he ordered the bishop
of London to call together all the clergy and tell them to
"inveigh vehemently and bitterly in they're sermons,
against the insolencie of our women" and women's wear-
ing of men's clothing (quoted in Woodbridge 1984, 143).[7]
The show opens with parodies of two popular tragedies.
The first, that of Hero and Leander, is a story of idealized—and unrequited—heterosexual love that Ovid re-
counts in *Heroides* (translated by Turbervile in 1567) and
which Marlowe retold in 1598. The second, the story of
Damon and Pythias, known through Richard Edwards's
rhymed play of 1571, is one of idealized homosexual
love. The toy seller Lanthorn Leatherhead says this story

... raises up the ghost of their friend Dionysius:
Not like a Monarch, but the Master of a Schoole,
In a Scriveners furr'd gowne, which shewes he is no
foole.
For therein he hath wit enough to keep himselfe
warme.
O Damon, *he cries, and* Pythias; *what harme,*
Hath poor Dionysius *done you in his grave* ... ?
(5.4.360–65)

The figure referred to is Dionysius the Elder (c. 430–367 BC), the tyrant of Syracuse who entered politics as a representative of the poor and who condemned Pythias (or Damon, the legend varies) to death for plotting against him. Pythias is given leave to arrange his affairs after Damon volunteers to give up his own life if Pythias does not return. Dionysius is so impressed by their love and devotion that he releases both of them and asks to be admitted to their brotherhood.

In *Bartholomew Fair* the puppet Dionysius also reflects the influence of the gender-blurring Greek god of the theater, Dionysus. In a dispute with the religious hypocrite Zeal-of-the-Land-Busy, he says his calling is "Of the Spirit" (5.5.60). Busy insists that his calling is profane, "as being the Page of *Pride*, and the waiting woman of *vanity*" (5.5.81–82). Leaping on the chance to invoke the tenuousness of gender distinctions, Dionysius asks Busy what he has to say regarding such women. Busy says he will not answer for them. Dionysius chides him for his refusal, stating that sin is something that people like Busy have within themselves, not something external like the clothes one wears. Can a puppet, who, after all, has no internal essence, be worse than this? Dionysius asks. "Yes," says Busy, "and my maine argument against you, is, that you are an *abomination*: for the Male, among you, putteth on the apparell of the *Female*, and the *Female* of the *Male*" (5.5.97–100). This, says Dionysius, *"is your old stale argument against the Players, but it will not hold against the Puppets; for we have neyther* Male *nor* Female *amongst us. And that thou may'st see, if thou wilt, like a malicious purblind zeale as thous art!"* (5.5.103–06). The puppet then lifts its garment and exposes itself.

This dramatic denial of gender distinctions, this denial of anatomical difference, and thus of gender, is also a representation of castration. By raising its garment, the puppet deliberately and pointedly exposes itself to the players and to us, the audience. This sudden unannounced gesture forces us to look, to gaze, at its *lack*. What we see is not a sign of sexual gender but, quite literally, nothing! That is, instead of revealing to us a hidden biological sign of sexual difference—a penis or a vagina—the puppet exposes an absence, a void. This not only denies the sign of the phallus, but also denies the forbidden site—and sight —of masculine desire that Courbet called *L'origine du monde.*

What we are forced to see, then, is that sexuality, like sin, is socially constructed through such signs as dress. This unveiling, this secularized apocalyptic scene, reveals nothing, exposing the idealist Platonic *mimesis* as empty and devoid of form. The scene therefore reaffirms our dependence on language as something more than merely the dress of thought. Language *constitutes* what we perceive as reality. What we assume to be true is always already contaminated by language, and this awareness breaks our mimetic dependence on sight as theatrical spectacle, as the ultimate upward displacement of sexuality. The puppet's exposure of its genderlessness, its neutrality, draws attention to the fact that all gender distinctions are in some sense theatrical representations, not essences.

By 1617, the increasingly problematic nature of desire had forced James to issue a declaration known as *The Book of Sports*, stating that people had to attend services on Sunday before they could engage in recreations. But this did not stem Puritan preachers' efforts to have such pastimes banned altogether. In the same year Prynne published his attack on the theater, 1633, Charles reissued

The Book of Sports and ordered it read in every parish church. Many Puritan ministers objected and refused to comply. Instead of seeing such mimetic, visceral, and carnivalesque pastimes as a "safety valve," a way for people to blow off steam on the Sabbath and therefore make it easier for them to work hard the rest of the week, some saw such pleasures as a direct threat to the development of the self-discipline and self-denial necessary for the accumulation of capital, which was identified in Calvinistic theology with the saving of one's soul.

The Sad Shepherd warns against the spread of this ethos into the countryside. In 1636 Jonson contributed "An Epigram to my Joviall Good friend *Mr. Robert Dover*, on his great Instauration of his Hunting, and Dauncing at *Cotswold*" to a collection of poems celebrating "the *Olympick Games*."[8] In an attempt to turn the table on the efforts of the rising middle classes to capture the center, the patriotic core of tradition, the poem maintains that these activities

> . . . advance true Love, and neighbourhood,
> And doe both *Church*, and Common-wealth the good,
> In spite of *Hipocrites*, who are the worst
> Of Subjects; Let such envie, till they burst.
> (*UV.* XLIII)

It is not cynicism to say that such an attempt was bound to fail. There could be no perception of a lack of continuity between past and present, between folk and courtly cultures, *unless* that rupture was already perceived to have occurred. I would argue that it has *always* already occurred.

Evidence of this hiatus, this gap, may be seen in *The Sad Shepherd* when Lionel makes no claim to moral perfection but says there is an important distinction between hypocrites who profess to be Christians while robbing people of their livelihoods and rural people who indulge in harmless sports. And he replies to Friar Tuck's lament over the business world's debasement of shepherding by sharp practice by explaining that such immorality is all the worse because it is hidden from view:

> O Friar, those are faults that are not seene;
> Ours open, and of worst example beene.
> They call ours, *Pagan* pastimes, that infect
> Our blood with ease, our youth with all neglect,
> Our tongues with wantonnesse, our thoughts with lust,
> And what they censure ill, all others must.
>
> (1.4.34–39)

The word "*Pagan*," i.e., non-Christian, is charged with political significance. It was a key term in the Sabbatarian Controversy and was prominent in Stubbes's *Anatomie*. Pastoral, as a vehicle for conveying the courtly culture's ideology, had traditionally served as a "middle-world pointing to the ultimate reconciliation of Pagan and Christian" (Hartman 1970, 189). Humanist intellectuals saw the newly literate middle classes as people who read their Bibles, as Christopher Hill has somewhat hyperbolically put it, "with no historical sense" (1967, 146). These intellectuals spoke in defense of what they believed was an older *oral* culture; through the study of Latin texts they had become cognizant of—indeed, they helped create—a gap between written and oral communication, which, in turn, fostered an awareness of a gulf between a thought or idea and its articulation.

Jonson's texts distance a version of himself from the urban, literate life of London. Jonas Barish has pointed out that Jonson often wrote about clothes and disguises "as a source of pleasure and a basis of identity," but at the same time he saw these things as "a mark of triviality, an addiction to the inessential and the transitory, as well as a futile and hence perverse attempt to rival nature" (1981, 150–51). Jonson's interest in the things that distinguish the high-born from the plebian—the scholar from the dunce—and his obsession with language—his insistence that it is not just the dress of thought, as Puritans would have it, but a determinant of social identity—derive from ambivalences within patriarchal culture. Such ambivalences are both produced by and produce a desire to let go to experience unrestrained bodily pleasure, and an opposing desire to restrain, to spiritualize and idealize the libido. Jonson's hostility toward the theatrical world, which Barish sees as a sign of a deep-seated personal anxiety about preserving "the primacy of the spoken word" (1981, 135), may also be seen as an effort to resist the totalizing tendencies of a fixed identity.

The absolutist ideal of wholeness and harmony created an awareness of social, as well as individual, fragmentation. This awareness manifested itself in Caroline pastoral as a nostalgia for what was seen, in retrospect, to be Elizabethan exuberance and was accompanied by a desire to flee, to escape from a debased and corrupting court. Such desire is reflected in the way in which *The Sad Shepherd* introduces the folk figures of Maid Marian and Robin Hood into courtly pastoral and affirms local traditions as part of an alternative culture that is allied with the natural order. But at the same time there is no attempt to imitate the language of the peasants, to reproduce the words or cadences of actual speech; instead Jonson resurrects phrases that had passed out of popular currency. The result is a kind of Brechtian alienation effect that plays off the remoteness of the written against the intimacy of colloquial speech. In this respect, the play may be said to revalue traditions of folk culture that had been appropriated by the courtly culture.

By not mentioning Robin Hood's alleged aristocratic background, the play rejects—or at least puts aside—the official depiction of the legendary outlaw, built up by Munday and others, as a heroic nobleman, a representative of the ruling elite, who descends for a brief time to the level of the people, thus demonstrating his and his class's solidarity with them by defying the hired officials of the ruling class and by tweaking the noses of the clerical elite who serve them. When George a Greene refers to the absent Robin Hood as "my Lord" (1.3.10), he recalls Robin Hood's role in Scotland as lord of the May Games and his association with the title of Lord of Misrule in the west Midlands, which Stubbes had described in his *Anatomie*. In such pageants, as a commoner elected to the temporary title of "Lord," Robin Hood parodied aristocratic manners and swaggering abuse of power; this, in turn, helped make politically subversive readings of the legend more plausible among the lower classes.

Sycophantic, opportunistic writers like Munday were encouraged to defuse the more dangerous and subversive aspects of the legend by blurring the class antagonism inherent in the legend, thus making the outlaw and his band palatable to *all* classes. In Munday's *Downfall*, for example, after 1,300 lines of tearful doggerel lamenting the loss of Robin Hood's aristocratic lifestyle and blaming those "hired to wrong a Nobleman" (l. 362), Matilda understandably yearns for a more pleasant future: "O God," she says to Robin Hood, "how full of perfect mirth were I,/ To see thy grief turnd to true jollitie!" To which Robin Hood swears:

> ... now gods curse on me light,
> If I forsake not grief, in griefes despight.
>   (ll. 1312–16)

They then attempt to dispel sadness with hollow laughter and begin a lengthy discussion about the proper way to address Robin Hood. Little John, who calls him "your Honour," is told to desist (ll. 1019–20), and Robin Hood punctiliously has a list of Articles drawn up and read aloud proclaiming "no man must presume to call our master,/ By name of Earle, Lord, Baron, Knight, or Squire." Yet no sooner has the list been read than all agree to "serve our master Robin Hood" (ll. 1329–33). Such irony, along with other references to Robin Hood's high social status, reconstitutes the gap separating him from ordinary people. In this way throughout the play, class distinctions are reaffirmed and an aura of nostalgia for an era that has been irrevocably lost is maintained.

In contrast to Munday's emphasis on Robin Hood as a representative of an imaginary past, Jonson's Robin Hood is historically ambiguous. The legendary outlaw's utopian vision of a future full of lovemaking and music is simultaneously both nostalgic and egalitarian. He sees no reason why the clock cannot be turned back and the country be

> (As 'twas) a happy age, when on the Plaines,
> The Wood-men met the Damsells, and the Swaines
> The Neat'ards, Plow-men, and the Pipers loud,
> And each did dance, some to the Kit, or Crowd,
> Some to the Bag-pipe, some the Tabret mov'd,
> And all did either love, or were belov'd.
> (1.4.42–47)

Lionel and Clarion agree that these innocent pleasures were enjoyed when shepherds "would sing" (1.4.49) and class antagonisms were nonexistent; no one mistrusted anyone else and "Shepherds knew how to love, and not to lust" (1.4.56). That is, they spontaneously and unselfconsciously enjoyed sensual pleasures because educated clerics had not yet taught them to wound their consciences with sinful thoughts. Therefore, instead of reaffirming the repressive hypothesis that Munday's Robin Hood does, Jonson's Robin Hood projects an idealized past into the future in precisely the way Bakhtin indicated carnival did—by presenting "the victory of the future, of the golden age, over the past" (1984, 256). Indeed, this utopian future is made to appear imminent. "Each minute that we loose thus," Clarion urges, "Deserves a censure on us, more or lesse" (1.4.57–58). And this shepherd, surprisingly aware of fleeting time, is sorry that Earine's loss has meant a diminishment "Both to the Mirth, and Musicke of this day" (1.4.60).

The chief redemptive instrument in this utopian vision, music, is further foregrounded by the rhyming couplets in which all of these speeches are cast. And the heavy endstops also call attention to the sound of the words. In this, the longest rhymed passage in the play, there are 35 couplets. Sixteen of them rhyme the same part of speech —e.g., fed/led, brock/flock, seen/been, etc. Such rhyming is characteristic of Chaucer and contrasts with the practice of Munday and most post-Restoration poets. Rhyming words that are the same parts of speech, as Antony Easthope has shown, calls attention to the rhyme and plays down the meaning. This emphasis on the sound of words acknowledges the dependence of meaning or content on style or form and denies priority to either.

> Such rhymes treat the signifier not as subordinate to the signified but rather as in a relationship of equality with it, so that they tend to coincide. Relative to subordination, coincidence in rhyme emphasizes the phonetic, so acknowledging the dependence of signified or signifier. In coincident rhyme, meaning is allowed to follow sound as much as sound does meaning; and the less *exact* the rhyme, the greater this effect (Easthope 1983, 90–91).

In act 1, scene 4 of *The Sad Shepherd*, the balance between weak rhymes, which are characteristic of older oral poetry, and strong ones, which become dominant in poetry intended to be read silently, also signifies momentary parity between spoken and written discourse, folk and courtly cultures, retrospective and progressive historical perspectives. Such parity also reflects an often noted ambivalence in Jonson's texts between an expressed desire to establish a fixed authorial presence—an individual transcendental ego—that controls and directs all discourse within a text and thus manipulates our responses, and an opposing desire—often implied—to set one's creations loose upon the world, to grant them autonomy and release them from authorial control. This helps explain why Jonson's plays and nondramatic poems frequently give the impression of impending chaos. We get the sense that Jonson is on the verge of abandoning the plot or losing control of the denouement, the story line that carries a conventional message reinforcing conventional morality and conventional "truth."

The stories Jonson's texts tell do not require readers to follow the thread of a plot or narrative. The resolution is decidedly *not* implicit in the presented situation. These stories picture the old hierarchical society, with its rigid class distinctions, in a process of dissolution. This perception of dissolution distances us from the characters and the situations being described. It forces us to establish distance between ourselves and an idealized past, as well as an apocalyptic future.

4

Unveiling the Phallus:
"Language most shewes a man"

MOROSE: Is that *Gorgon*, that *Medusa*, come?
Hide me, hide me!
TRUEWIT: I warrant you, sir,
she will not transform you.
Look upon her with good courage—

Epicoene (3.7.21–25)

To conceptualize the formation of levels of culture, Dominick LaCapra has suggested that

The distinction among popular, mass, and elite (or high) culture seems to parallel and in certain respects may shape Freud's topology of id, ego, superego. Particularly in the late sixteenth and seventeenth centuries in Europe, elite culture . . . became . . . aligned with official state culture in a hegemonic formation that . . . tried to establish a shared superego (1989, 58).

I would supplement this formulation by suggesting that, in Lacanian terms, folk culture corresponds to the Real, courtly or "high" culture corresponds to the Imaginary, and popular culture to the Symbolic. That is to say, the linkage between these three cultures is synchronic rather than diachronic. Just as the Real, Imaginary, and Symbolic work together in adult life to coordinate acts of psychic consciousness, conceptions of folk, courtly, and popular culture work together in modern society to coordinate acts of cultural consciousness.

In the *Sad Shepherd* the absence of any reference to Robin Hood's alleged noble background and the presence of witchcraft mark this text as a signifier of popular culture. The absence signals a coincidence of folk and courtly cultures even while it marks them as anachronistic, as existing retrospectively, but understood through the process that Freud called *Nachträglichkeit,* deferred action.[1] This absence of noble background also marks an erasure of the phallic function, of paternity, of patriarchy, and of a concept of masculinity that is always already lapsed, always already longing to fulfil itself and regain a lost wholeness. The presence of witchcraft, on the other hand, signals the fearful immanent—and monstrous—birth of a new bastard or oxymoronic popular culture out of the womb of a Mother Nature whose sexuality is no longer under the control of patriarchy.

Virtually all of the characters in *The Sad Shepherd* resist the values associated with the new, Puritan, urban, middle-class popular culture. For example, after Robin Hood expresses his longing to recapture the ideal organic community represented by music, dancing, and outdoor lovemaking, he repeats the warning given him by the sage Alken (all-seeing, all-knowing), Jonson's persona in the play (*Conv.* 394), that they should indulge Aeglamour's passion for his lost Earine

> For Phant'sie stop't, will soone take fire, and burne
> Into an anger, or to a Phrensie turne.
> (1.4.77–78)

Aeglamour's self-absorption results in a form of madness which is like that of Empedocles who leaped into the volcano because the public would not recognize him as a god (see Jonson's translation of Horace's *Art of Poetry* ll. 659–69). The abduction of his mistress blinds him to everything and everyone else. And this blindness takes a peculiarly contradictory form.

In conventional pastoral poetry, as in Spenser's *Colin Clouts come home againe* (1595), the eponymous shepherd says that at the urban court of Cynthia, love is blasphemed; so he will return to the countryside where he will carve Cynthia's

> . . . name on every tree . . .
> That as the trees do grow, her name may grow:
> And in the ground each where will it engrosse,
> And fill with stones, that all men it know.
>
> (ll. 632–35)

Here Platonic love is the divine power that surpasses reason; it draws opposites together, makes cold covet heat, water want fire, and emptiness seek satiety. Out of the fruitful womb of the great mother, this earth is born and all the creatures on it; and these creatures, like the engendering divine masculine power, desire to beget others like themselves. Human beings alone have the spark of reason to rule their passions. Those who do not rule their passion with reason "Are outlawes, . . ./ For their desire is base, and doth not merit,/ The name of love, but of disloyal lust" (890–92).

The Sad Shepherd contradicts and therefore challenges this Platonic genderization of the universe. Maid Marian and Robin Hood most certainly do not rule their passions with reason. They do not even recognize such strictures. They are both clearly outlaws in a more profound sense than the conventional one, and their outlawry infects the pastoral shepherds. For example, unlike a conventional shepherd who lives in concordance with nature's laws, Aeglamour expresses a desire to *control* nature, to dominate it and convert it into a book that tells no story but that of his lost love. He wishes to violate the official view that God made his intentions known through nature, that he was present in nature in the same way that people were present in their bodies. In his wish to imprint his self-absorbed plan for vengeance on nature, Aeglamour expresses a desire to usurp that Godlike presence; he wants to overwrite his own obsessive and unnuanced text *on* nature, an act that will cancel out, or at least confute, the ambiguous hieroglyphic God inscribed *in* nature.

He vows "An exquisite revenge" (1.5.2), swears Robin Hood and the shepherds to silence, and announces that he will carve his plan for vengeance

> . . . on the trees, and in the turfe,
> On every greene sworth, and in every path,
> Just to the Margin of the cruell *Trent*;
> There will I knock the story in the ground,
> In smooth great peble, and mosse-fill it round,
> Till the whole Countrey read how she was drown'd.
> (1.5.5–10)

In his solipsistic fantasy, the body of Mother Nature becomes a passive receptor of his desire for revenge. He finds no solace in this body. He does not listen to it or read it, thus he cannot learn from it; he merely wishes to exploit it, to make it fit his needs, his purposes. Instead of regarding nature as a text through which God-the-teacher both speaks and inscribes his message, Aeglamour, more complusively than Spenser's Colin, reverses the platitude Francis Quarles set down in his pious *Emblems* in 1635:

> The world's a book in folio, printed all
> With God's great works in letters capital.
> (quoted in Curtius 323)

Thus, not all instances of the book-of-nature topos are the same. As Derrida has pointed out

> the most decisive separation appears at the moment when, at the same time as the science of nature, the determination of absolute presence is constituted as self-presence,

as subjectivity. It is the moment of the great rationalisms of the seventeenth century. From then on, the condemnation of fallen and finite writing will take another form, within which we still live: it is non-self-presence that will be denounced. (1977, 16–17)

Like the speaker in Marvell's "The Garden," who articulates a desire to free consciousness from the veil of textuality and make it present to itself in the light of reason, Aeglamour inverts official religious hierarchies through his "heresy," as he himself calls it. This demonstrates how Robin Hood's bower functions as a setting for a ritualized displacement of the identity between ideology and culture. Aeglamour's myopic, excessive—and therefore unmanly—grief causes him to assume that the illiterate peasants of the countryside surrounding Sherwood Forest, the inhabitants of that marginal agrarian region that is neither part of the urban culture nor part of the uncultivated and pristine world of the greenwood, not only can but want to "read how [Earine] was drown'd" (1.5.10). By reading about her loss they will somehow, magically, learn how to "alter the complexion of the Spring" (1.5.12). He believes that by learning to read the text he imprints on nature, the peasants will cease to be passive agents of nature. Instead of being acted upon by this maternal body, they will manipulate it and change the cyclic pattern of the seasons.

These blatant attempts to subvert nature's course, and thus God's purposes, call attention to the gap between human desires and nature's actions; this awareness, in turn, prepares the way for the consideration of alternatives to the official view of eschatology throughout the Middle Ages. Aeglamour's madness places him outside of, and in opposition to, the old alchemical view of nature. Aeglamour does not read the book of nature in accordance with the typological hermeneutics of scriptural exegesis, which was taught in the medieval refectory under the tutelage of a clerical elite but which was, in the Renaissance, consigned to cranks. Instead, he wishes to inscribe his own idosyncratic desire for revenge, which is antifeminine in the sense that it is a displaced desire for revenge against the mother for abandoning him, on the body of the ultimate mother, nature. His wish for total autonomy, like that of Faustus and those Renaissance men he represents and whose desires he epitomizes, reverses the traditional relationship between humans and nature, and betrays a desire to play God.

Spinoza termed this desire the *causa sui* project. As the medieval organic view of nature was displaced by the Renaissance empirical view, there was an attempt to create what Susan Bordo has called a " 'story' of *parturition.*" That is, what was seen as the painful psychological process of separation from the mother was expressed "in anxiety over the *enclosedness* of the individual self, the isolating uniqueness of each individual allotment by an alien, indifferent universe." In this way an empirical view of nature was seen in light of this "*cultural* separation anxiety," as symptomatic of "an aggressive intellectual *flight* from the female cosmos and 'feminine' orientation towards the world," which was "decisively purged from the dominant intellectual culture, through the Cartesian 'rebirthing' and restructuring of knowledge and world as *masculine*" (Bordo 1987, 100).

But Aeglamour's view of nature is clearly not yet purged of maternal associations. He says that if his first attempt to usurp divinity does not work he will invert nature in yet another way. He "will get some old, old Grandam" (1.5.13) and, by placing her foot in the river Trent, will cause the water to become ice; it will "loose all vertue" (1.5.16), that is, all its life-giving properties, its ability to nurture the growth of the crops that the peasants depend upon for their livelihoods. If this invocation of feminine sexual frigidity does not assuage his overheated masculine anger, he will invert the river's lifegiving properties in another way: "when the year's at hottest,/ . . . [he will] . . . fling a fellow with a Fever in,/ To set it all on fire, till it burne,/ Blew as *Scamander*, 'fore the walls of *Troy*" (1.5.20–25).

Such hyperbolic threats violate the conventionally placid tone of pastoral and emphasize its fragility and superficiality; this, in turn, brings to our attention the vulnerability of the courtly values that pastoral traditionally conveyed. The fact that such violent language is uttered by a lowly shepherd subverts the assumed social hierarchies whereby the strongest language is reserved for the ostensible hero, Robin Hood. And Aeglamour's call for the violation of nature, which challenges the stability of the social as well as the natural world, is part of a larger process, whereby appeals to God in support of an immutable and unalterable social hierarchy are replaced by appeals to nature.

Robin Hood follows Alken's advice and congratulates Aeglamour for his "just revenge/ Which . . . is so perfect" (1.5.29–30). But Aeglamour continues in a melancholy fit that rivals—indeed parodies—the excessive despair Jonson said Donne had expressed over the loss of Elizabeth Drury (*Conv.* 43–48). "Did not the whole Earth sicken, when she died?" Aeglamour asks (1.5.37). And to Karolin's song about Love's ability to kill through heat as well as Death's through cold, he replies:

> Doe you thinke so? are you in that good heresie?
> I meane opinion? If you be, say nothing:
> I'll study it, as a new Philosophy.
>
> (1.5.81–83)

The self-correction of "heresie" to "opinion" calls attention to the unconventionality of Karolin's sentiment. And Aeglamour's equation of the seemingly slight lyric Karolin has sung to something as grandly intellectual as the "new Philosophy"—the theories of Galileo and Kepler—is so outlandishly hyperbolic that it requires us to consider in what sense Aeglamour, who is mad with grief and can therefore say anything, is guilty of saying something profane and blasphemous.

The passage subverts the conventions of pastoral and directs attention to them as cultural constructions. Just as empirical science called all traditional knowledge of the external natural world into question, the reference to this new way of thinking, this divorce of the material from the spiritual, implies that the pastoral conventions, and therefore the values that they conveyed, are also vulnerable. And to reinforce this skepticism about pastoral conventions, *The Sad Shepherd* here mocks a scene from other pastoral plays such as Rutter's *Shepherd's Holy-day*, where Nerina upbraids Hylas for having once stolen a kiss from her, by having Aeglamour force Amie to kiss Karolin. If Earine were alive, he says, "you should have twenty:/ For every line here" (1.5.87–88). Here again an awareness of textuality, of literariness, obtrudes into the *mimesis*; for what shepherd, even in the most self-consciously crafted pastoral, would intrude the fact that he is speaking lines? And, as if this were not enough to drive home the point, Clarion recalls "The Lovers Scriptures" and names several writers of Greek romances. Reinforcing his role as an authorial persona, Alken comments that he has "knowne some few,/ And read of more." Lionel finally calls a halt to this digression on the artificial and bookish qualities of pastoral—and therefore of the play itself—by asking a devastatingly apt question: "what is this/ To jolly *Robin*?" (1.5.96–101).

What indeed! And why is such a digression obtruding into what has been assumed to be a conventional pastoral play, undermining the mimetic effect of the entire performance? One answer is that it is pointing to a new self-consciousness of the textuality of the drama, to the awareness of a text as the "source" of what happens on the stage, and to the playwright as the author of that text—a writer whose interior life, whose consciousness, is present on the stage in the voices he provides for his characters. Alken's speech calls attention to the idea that the poetic act of creation, of personification, has taken place before and apart from the public appearance on the stage where the character's words are spoken as though they were extemporaneous. Jonson, as the prototypical poet/

writer/editor, has become sensitized—and therefore wishes to sensitize his audience—both to the invisibility of his text and to the hidden, interior space of his self. As the Oxford editors remark, "Pastoral orthodoxy held that 'the truest Lovers are least fortunate,' and recited 'Lovers Scriptures' to prove it; 'jolly Robin' defies such augury" (H&S 2.228). And in so doing, Robin makes the aristocratic world of pastoral look artificial and foreign. Along with Maid Marian and his band, he stands for "simple loves, and sampled lives" (1.5.110). Together, their virtue is better envied than pitied, for "wretched pitty ever cals on scornes" (1.5.114).

So here we have representatives of a folk culture, which is supposedly struggling on the edges of extinction, who are bravely rejecting the nostalgic sentimentality and patronizing attitudes of courtly culture. And to further dramatize this defiance and resistance to cooption, Maid Marian kills the king's deer and brings it home as bounty for Robin Hood and his band. She joyously kisses him and delightedly describes how she hunted and slew the "lusty Stagge" (1.6.22). Like Sir Gawain's host, she did it properly, according to the unwritten rules of masculine sportsmanship, the tribal encyclopaedia of hunting lore passed down orally throughout the Middle Ages and recorded in handbooks such as the anonymous *Le Livre de Chasse du Roy Modus* and George Tubervile's *Noble Arte of Venerie or Hunting* (1575), which Jonson evidently consulted for his description.[2]

In the play this ritualized hunt and ceremonial slaughter is not without an ominous aspect, for as it was taking place a raven—which, in the alchemical tradition is associated with melancholia—sat croaking and crying overhead. This is the same bird the first Hag in *The Masque of Queenes* witnessed all day "feeding upon a Quarter;/ And, soone as she turn'd her beake to ye *South*,/ I snatch'd this morsal out of her Mouth" (ll. 155–58). The threatening presence of this melancholy bird— who is, as the huntsmen suspect, an incarnation of the sorrowful witch Mother Maudlin, whom Scathlock met at dawn "just as hee rows'd the Deere" (1.6.48)—draws attention to the ominousness of the gender inversion evoked by Maid Marian's hunting and slaying of the deer.

Ravens were often associated with witchcraft and with the abuse of dead bodies, as in Lucan's *Erichtho*, which Jonson cites in his extensive notes to *The Masque of Queenes* (see H&S 7.290n1, and also notes on 292, 294–95). In the ballad called "The Three Ravens" (Child 1.26A), published by Thomas Ravenscroft in *Melismata* in 1611, ravens contemplate eating the corpse of a slain knight whose hounds and hawks guard his corpse until a pregnant doe kisses his wounds and properly buries him before she herself expires. Thus the ballad, like Jonson's play, contains an idealized version of the social hierarchy as the ruling classes might wish to see it; this point of view is contradicted from the point of view of the peasantry by the ravens.

Easthope has observed that in the ballad "the birds of carrion and the sympathetic death of the pregnant doe link the death of the knight to a generalized sterility (983, 83). If we apply the Freudian concept of compromise-formation, we could say that the knight stands for the father and the doe for the mother. Contradictory attitudes toward the father are represented, the wish to submit (the hounds and the hawks) and the wish to castrate and/or kill (the ravens). Such an explanation, as Lacan explains, shows how "the signifying chain of a discourse," which is constructed in a unified linearity, closes meaning and offers a coherent position to the subject—a fixed position for the ego as "a single voice" (1957, 154). But as Easthope explains, "There is progression and coherence in the syntagmatic chain of 'Three Ravens' but no attempt to close the chain tightly. . . . Parataxis leaves the text open" (1983, 87–88).

In his essay entitled "Guiding Remarks for a Congress on Feminine Sexuality," Lacan observed that

> if there is no virility which castration does not consecrate, then for the woman it is a castrated lover or a dead man (or even both at the same time) who hides behind the veil

where he calls on her adoration from that same place beyond the maternal *imago* which sent out the threat of a
castration not really concerning her. (1982, 95)

Like the dead knight in "The Three Ravens," Robin Hood
is a passive lover, and as such he is a son, not a father. Ma-
rian/Maudlin is a Janus-faced lover-mother, as the names
Marian and Maudlin represent two opposed forms of
femininity, the Virgin Mary and Mary Magdalene. (Magdalene and Maudlin are homonyms in most spoken dia-
lects in Britain.) Robin Hood's band, as well as peasants
such as Scathlock, are other "sons" who express hostility
toward Alken, an Apollonian father figure who represents
moderation, restraint, and fear of castration. If we read the
remaining scenes of the play in this light, we can further
explore ways in which the Oedipal triangle produces and
is produced by gendered subjectivity.

For example, when squeamish Amie refuses to go see
the slain deer, Mellifleur tries to cheer her up by telling
her "wee will eate him merrily" (1.6.55). Wise Alken
immediately senses trouble and asks Scathlock, who is
not a pastoral shepherd but a local peasant, if he saw the
raven. Scathlock replies in a broad Yorkshire or Low Scots
dialect.[3] By its defamiliarization of ordinary speech, this
dialect calls attention to the gap between the speech of
the upper classes and that of marginalized peasants and
highlights the fact that Scathlock's answer is curiously
hostile even when stripped of the dialect and translated
into modern English. Scathlock says: "I, qu'ha suld let
me?/ I suld be afraid o' you, sir, suld I? (1.6.56–57), meaning: "Yes, I saw it. Who would stop me? Surely you
couldn't, now could you?" This use of dialect again foregrounds the idea that language is the determinant of
social status, and it also signifies the demise of the social acceptance of such forms of speech in the new urban
middle-class business world.

Scathlock's utterance is a hostile speech spoken in a
crude dialect by a person of low social standing to one of
higher social standing, a representative of high culture.
Clarion is shocked by the implications of Scathlock's

speech and upbraids him for not showing proper respect for his betters. But then something even more curious happens. Robin Hood interrupts Clarion and tells him to stop. "You must give them all their rudenesse," he says. "They are not else themselves, without their language" (1.6.59–60). He maintains, in other words, that the peasants' speech defines them properly, as they truly are, not as they should be or as others might wish them to be.

This scene, then, dramatizes the radical inversion of values whereby language—not dress, not manners, and especially not heredity—defines one's social position. And this inversion, like Maid Marian instead of Robin Hood slaying the deer, conforms to neither aristocratic nor middle-class hierarchies. It stands on the margin of both of those contending discourses in the same way that the world of folk culture stands on the margin of the two warring cultures—aristocratic and Puritan—of Caroline England. Jonson, we may recall, believed that Spenser had made a mistake in attempting to imitate ancient speech (*Disc.* 1806–07) and that Sidney had erred in making all his characters speak like aristocrats (*Conv.* 17–19). He further believed that natural language had been corrupted by the habit of twisting it and torturing it, embroidering it, powdering and painting it like a made up face, and he especially accused noblemen of this vice. "Nothing is fashionable," he wrote,

> till it bee deform'd; and this is to write like a *Gentleman*. All must bee as affected, and preposterous as our Gallants cloathes, sweet bags, and night-dressings . . . . Wheresoever, manners, and fashions are corrupted, Language is. It imitates the publicke riot. The excesses of Feasts, and apparell, are all the notes of a sick State; and the wantonnesse of language, of a sick mind (*Disc.* 582–85, 954–56).[4]

In an effort to situate the medium of the professional writer in the social stratum, Jonson said that language belonged to the people, not to the Latinists and grammarians; playwrights should therefore have their character's speak according to their social position (*Disc.* 1889–94).

Employing a simile that connects the idea of language as a compromise-formation, a form of magic—or, as Wittgenstein, following Plato, would have it, of bewitchment—and that pictures money as heir to and substitute for God —as the filthy lucre of the Devil—Jonson declared that "*Custome* is the most certaine Mistress of Language, as the publicke stampe makes the current money" (*Disc.* 1926). Yet he also expressed the traditional humanist fear that if the consent of the learned were abandoned "wee should speake or live after the manners of the vulgar" (*Disc.* 1941-42), an attitude based on the assumption that language is a political thing, a determinant of reality in the Whorfian sense. His statement that "Language most shewes a man: speake that I may see thee" (*Disc.* 2331-32) undermines the link between Renaissance humanism and the privileging of vision as it downgrades dress and manners, things we can see, as the criteria of social standing. And the idea that language "springs out of the most retired, and inmost parts of us, and is the Image of the Parent of it, the mind" (*Disc.* 2032–33), is an example of the logocentric, and classically Platonic, proposition that there is an abstract realm of ideas that exists prior to their articulation in language.

Indeed, as Jonson explains, it is the "aptness" of language, not its conformity to a hierarchical standard of correctness, that determines its value, its usefulness. There is, then, no fixed, objective standard of the best way to speak or write. The best language allows people to "calmely study the separation of opinions, find the errours [that] have intervened, awake Antiquity, [and] call former times into question; but," he cautions, language should "make no parties with the present" (*Conv.* 2107–10); that is, its proper use should not be determined by any one group or class. It should be used to dissect social ills and moral obtuseness, not to smooth over class conflicts and contradictions. Similarly, in *The English Grammar* Jonson resisted the idea that English should be modeled on Latin. Following Peter Ramus, he called for the reshaping of "naturall, and home-borne words, which though in number they be not many, . . . yet in variation are so divers, and uncertaine, that they need much the stampe of some good *Logick*, to beat them into proportion" (chap. 18.6–10).

Of course, Renaissance drama itself repeatedly invites reflection upon the meaning of individual identity, but *The Sad Shepherd* places the audience's complicity in the deception in question. Renaissance drama may, as Stephen Greenblatt has observed, celebrate "the successful insertion of one individual into the identity of another," but it does not "inevitably" expose "the mechanisms of imposture" (1986, 219). *The Sad Shepherd* dramatizes the fact that language is always a problematic means of defining oneself and of maintaining one's identity.

No sooner has Mother Maudlin been introduced then the question of her "true" identity arises. Scathlock says: "They call her a Wise-woman, but I thinke her/ An arrant Witch" (1.6.62–63). The question of who "they" are who think her wise is left unanswered. In no other play in which witches had appeared—including George Gifford's *Dialogue Concerning Witches* (1593); Shakespeare's *1 Henry VI* (1592–94), where Joan of Arc appears as a witch; *Macbeth* (1604); *The Tempest* (1610); John Marston's *The Wonder of Woman or the Tragedy of Sophonisba* (1606); Thomas Middleton's *The Witch* (c. 1616); William Rowley, Thomas Dekker, and John Ford's *The Witch of Edmonton* (acted 1621; printed 1658); and Thomas Heywood and Richard Brome's *The Late Lancashire Witches* (1634)—is the identity of a real or supposed witch so problematized.

To settle the matter of Marian/Maudlin's identity, Robin Hood calls for Marian, but when she appears she only further complicates the question of authentic identity, for now, possessed by the witch Mother Maudlin, she has completely changed her character. All her former characteristics—warmth, affection, charm, humor, spontaneity—are gone, and she appears as a cold, temperamental, calculating and snobbish shrew who orders the slain deer sent to herself, accuses Robin Hood of spying on her, disparages the peasants' simple fare, and makes fun of their tawdry festival. After he sees the results of this transformation of Maid Marian into a Terrible Mother, Robin Hood fears his own senses have deceived him, for in outward appearance and speech the witch appears to be his beloved Maid Marian, but her actions and words are totally out of character.[5]

This transformation in the key feminine figure in the play puts into question Robin Hood's role as a transgressive, carnivalesque figure. At first "Maid" Marian was the chaste lover; she stood outside of society's stereotypical feminine role model that leads from virginity to married chastity. She killed the king's deer and freely made love with the outlawed Robin Hood. But her transformation by the spirit of "Mother" Maudlin turns her into a maenad, a bacchanalian female whose rebellion against male dominance is more ominous that anything Robin Hood previously suspected. His naïveté is apparent when he asks the others if they notice these changes, but then, upon reflection, he turns the question around: "Are wee not all chang'd/ Transformed from our selves?" he asks. "I do not know!" Lionel replies thoughtfully, "The best is silence!" (1.7.33–37)

This echo of Hamlet's final words—"the rest is silence" (5.2.359)—implies that there is nothing more to say. There is nothing more that speech can accomplish. The rest is writing. Hamlet, the most longwinded character in Renaissance drama, finally articulates an idea that has been implicit since the beginning of the play: that copious living speech—which both in the play and in the discourse of the time (as satirized in *Epicoene*) is associated with femininity—is silenced by action. Lionel's echo suggests that when confronted by an evil feminine figure such as Mother Maudlin, it is *best* for men to remain silent.[6] Hamlet has at last *acted*, as a *man* (as opposed to speaking, as a woman); he has fulfilled the demand of his father that he conform to the traditional masculine stereotype and revenge his murder. He asserts the identity of life and speech with the Name-of-the-Father, the transcendental phallic signifier. His last breath, his expiration, is the consummation of his long-delayed action; he has ceased to produce the living breath that transports speech, which is the producer of meaningful action. He has reached an end of his effort to revenge his father's murder, to live up to his name, to justify his existence and explain everything to himself and to the world.

If one does not know, cannot "fix," one's identity, define one's sexuality, it is "best" to remain silent. "The paradigm, for the subversion of identity is . . . the confusion of gender" (Guillory 1986, 114). Claudius, we may recall, charges Hamlet with "unmanly grief" (1.2.94). Nietzsche's characterization of Hamlet as a Dionysian figure in *The Birth of Tragedy* (sec. 7) points to a similar blurring of his gender identity, and Freud's labeling him a "hysteric" in *The Interpretation of Dreams* (1955d, 264–66), confirms this.[7] Thus we can say that Lionel's intertextual echo of Hamlet's final words evokes the consequences of a failure to control certain aspects of feminine sexuality. And this further suggests that Robin Hood's seduction by Maid Marian means that he—like so many other men—has succumbed to women's wiles, has been taken away from his public vocation and made a captive of the domestic realm. When Maid Marian kills the deer and delivers it to Robin Hood, she is assuming the masculine position of power. Robin Hood is left in the traditionally feminine position of domestic—and sexual—passivity. But this is only temporary, for Mother Maudlin's transformation of Maid Marian destroys the inverted hierarchy of her domestic relationship with Robin Hood. Alken, the symbolic father, sees to that.

The evocation of these meanings in Lionel's speech suggests the same bit of folk wisdom Peer Gynt arrives at as he peels a wild onion—there is no kernel of individual identity at the heart of everyman (or everywoman); the idea of a fixed personal self is paradoxical because, according to Christian theology, to be one's self one must slay one's self. As Robin Hood sees, it is not just Maid Marian who has changed; everyone has been transformed from their former selves. The "best" thing to do under such circumstances—from the point of view of the established order—is to keep quiet, to control one's tongue, and, as Alken, a spokesman for the patriarchal social order, says in language that points to the underlying sexual displacement, "await the issue." But even here Robin Hood contradicts him: "The dead, or lazie wait for't," he says, "I will find it" (1.7.37–38).

This is something more than just a criticism of Alken's passivity; it is a negation as well of Hamlet's solipsistic implication that his death, his silence, evokes the coming apocalypse, as prefigured in the description in 2 Esdras 7.26–36, a passage his words echo. In Jonson's play, Lionel's re-echo of those words evokes the world of Hamlet as a pretext that has been superseded. For just as Hamlet stands in opposition to the courtier tradition represented by Laertes, Rosencrantz, Guildenstern, and the sycophantic Osric, Jonson's evocation of the English folk hero offers a commentary on and provides an alternative to the courtly society whose ethos was embodied in the ideal of pastoral romance. Lionel's substitution of "best" for Hamlet's "rest" shifts the implication from temporal closure to optimistic expectation. The coming apocalypse is not, as Hamlet imagines, an end to history; it is only an end to history as he has known it. The apocalyptic expectation harbors the prospect, however mythical, of a new beginning.

The paradoxical search for "true" identity is revealed in the second act of Jonson's play, as disguises are stripped away. We open on a scene where Mother Maudlin gloats to her daughter Douce over her successful disturbance of the sexually explicit love between Robin Hood, whom she likens to a "vauting hart," and Marian, "his venting hind" (2.1.13). Speaking in a northern dialect, Maudlin tells Douce that by dressing in Earine's garments she may now seduce Aeglamour because the real Earine is, like the nymph Daphne who fled from Apollo, locked in an oak tree as a prize for her son Lorel, who is dressed "like a Prince/ Of Swine'aerds!" (2.1.34–35; cf. *A Midsummer Night's Dream* 2.1.230–34, and Marvell's "The Garden" 11. 27–32). The line break, which turns the phrase into an oxymoron, reverses the association we have just been asked to make between Lorel and nobility and prepares us to consider Lorel's ambiguous social status.

Unlike Shakespeare's Caliban, who is cut off from his own culture and who rejects Prospero's attempts to nurture him, Lorel is ungallant and ignoble, but lacks neither cultural refinement nor wealth. Far from being a cultural outcast or an outlaw, he perfectly represents the new vulgar man in the seventeenth century countryside, the agricultural entrepreneur. He merely pretends not to understand why the ingénue, Earine, is repulsed by his uncourtly and therefore grotesque appearance, his satyrlike pug nose, thick lips, and bristled chin. He knows very well that he does not fit the stereotype of the handsome courtier, but he also knows that that stereotype is outmoded. He knows that history is on his side; he is a rich man who has bought great tracts of land and who owns much livestock. He himself does no physical labor but, like the classical Theocritus whom he has read about, sits in the shade of a poplar tree all day playing the shepherd's pipe. He offers to play for Earine, but she declares all minstrelry irksome and spurns his gifts of small animals because they might ruin her clothes. The effect of these as well as other aspects of the scene is to render the audience's perception of Lorel totally ambivalent. For at the beginning of the scene the audience has been prepared not to like him. He is, after all, the son of an ugly and hateful witch who keeps poor Earine stocked up in a tree. But less than 50 lines later he is seen as a well-to-do gentleman-farmer whose tender gift of small cuddly animals is rejected by a prim and snobbish young woman afraid to soil her petticoats.

This does not necessarily mean that Jonson was sympathetic to the rackrenting agricultural landlords, but it does suggest that he was aware of how preconceptions about social position were becoming problematic. In other words, changing socioeconomic conditions had so upset the hierarchical social standards of class that this rupture was part of Jonson's perception of social conditions. Lorel's behavior parodies that of the conventional pastoral shepherd-lover who represented the values of the courtly elite. But here in Robin Hood's bower where Lorel is removed from the conventions of courtly society, the significance of his social ambivalence is revealed. For by attempting to disguise his plebian social background with fancy clothes and refined tastes, he points up the social ambivalence at the heart of Caroline society. And just as that ambivalence unmasks the material basis of his privileged social position, it empties the assumptions of those who look down upon him of any rational content and exposes that emptiness.

Earine too is a kind of mock-shepherdess. Instead of defending—and therefore identifying herself with—natural moderation, as pastoral shepherdesses such as the Lady in Milton's *Comus* (1634) had traditionally done, she refuses the gift of animals and shows overmuch concern for her dress, the sign of her social status. Her virtue is thereby trivialized and made to appear merely squeamish; her reluctance to embrace Lorel is a result of fastidiousness rather than self-respect. When she rejects Lorel's gift, she mockingly echoes his rustic dialect in an attempt to disparage his lower-class origins and his lack of sophistication. But of course this appears to be motivated by mere snobbishness; it is certainly not conduct becoming a pastoral shepherdess, a representative of the courtly elite.

To further emphasize Lorel's ambivalent social position, his mother, Maudlin, and his sister, Douce, scorn him as unmanly for wooing Earine with animals. Maudlin says he should have given her a barn-owl because "then/ Tho' hadst made a present o' thy selfe, Owle-spiegle!" (2.3.9–10) This pun on the name of the northern German folk hero Till Eulenspiegel—who, like Robin Hood, was well known for the practical jokes he played on clerics—

is yet another example of how references to folk culture throughout the play lower or debase pastoral conventions. To drive home the point, Maudlin tells her son that instead of offering Earine small animals he should have presented her

> . . . with mare pleasand things,
> Things naturall, and what all woemen covet
> To see: the common Parent of us all!
> Which Maids will twire at, 'tween their fingers, thus!
> With which his Sire gat him! Hee's gett another!
> And so beget posteritie upon her!
>
> (2.3.14–19)

This speech shocks us into an awareness of a social reality previously hidden behind the fragile mask of pastoral conventions. That a mother should taunt her son with the blatant statement that a gift of animal cubs is unpleasant and unnatural, and that what a refined young woman would like is for him to expose his penis so she can fondle it, and for a mother to tell her son that he is not a man unless he seduces this young woman of high social standing, is not only an unexpected inversion of pastoral convention and a profound debasement of the mores of supposedly polite society, but it is also an emblematic exposure of the central symbol of that society, the phallus. In Maudlin's profane speech, the phallocentrism of courtly culture is unveiled, stripped of its mystification under pastoral discourse.

What is more, Maudlin's threat to strip her son of his fancy clothes if he fails to seduce Earine is parodic of the conduct of courtly culture, for those clothes are Lorel's entree into that culture in the same way that Earine's clothes are for Douce. Mother Maudlin thus exposes a contradiction in courtly culture when she tells Douce to show herself boldly among the shepherds and tell them Maudlin gave her the clothes. This, she says, will so frighten them that Maudlin will easily "pu' the world, or Nature, 'bout their eares" (2.3.35). In other words, seeing that a witch is able to capture one of their own, strip her of her identity, and impose that identity upon another will show the shepherds—as well as us—that Maudlin knows their social position is fragile. Simultaneously, this demonstrates the shallowness of such class distinctions, thereby sharpening awareness of the vulnerability, the instability and the lack of any basis in "nature" for these distinctions. This awareness of the fragility of identity is further dramatized by an announcement that Maudlin herself can assume so many shapes that she can only be known to her daughter by a belt embroidered with mysterious hieroglyphics that a gypsy made for her under the watchful eyes of Hecate.

Hecate, of course, was a well-known embodiment of feminine evil. In his notes to *The Masque of Queenes*, Jonson himself had traced her lineage and had shown how, in their appropriation of folk traditions, ancient authors such as Euripides, Virgil, Ovid, and Seneca had transformed the fertility goddess into the figure of Hecate and divided her into three aspects: in her heavenly guise she is Phoebe or Cynthia, on earth she is Artemis (Diana) or Lucina, and in hell she is Proserpina—or simply Hecate herself. In *A Midsummer Night's Dream*, Puck refers to "triple Hecate's team (5.1.386); in *Hamlet*, Lucianus refers to "Hecate's ban thrice blasted, thrice infected" (3.2.264); Macbeth speaks of witchcraft celebrating "Pale Hecate's offerings" (2.1.52) and of "black Hecate's summons" (3.2.4), and it is Hecate herself who foretells Macbeth's fate (3.5.21ff). Lear, too, swears by her mysteries (1.1.110).

In Middleton's *The Witch*, Hecate upbraids her son Firestone for his desire to sleep with "a fat parson's daughter" rather than with her (1.2.92). A major subtext of this play, which appropriates material from Jonson's *Masque of Queenes*,[8] is the most sensational scandal of the Jacobean era, which I alluded to briefly in the second chapter —Lady Frances Howard's trial and conviction for poisoning Sir Thomas Overbury. In the trial it was revealed that Lady Frances, along with her serving woman Mrs. Anne

Turner, had consulted the astrologer/magician/alchemist Simon Forman (1552–1611).[9] In Middleton's play, the gender of the occult figure, Forman, is changed. The Lady Frances figure, Isabella, consults with Hecate, who prepares a potion for her made of bear-breech, lizard's-brain, and "three ounces of the red-hair'd girl/ I kill'd last midnight" (5.2.55–56).

The Sad Shepherd is in many ways a reply to Middleton's play. Jonson told Drummond he thought Middleton a "base fellow" (*Conv.* 167–68) and called Overbury his "mortall enemie" (*Conv.* 170). He also reported that Overbury had asked him to help him in his seduction of Lady Frances's aunt, Sir Philip Sidney's daughter, Elizabeth, whom Jonson said wrote poetry not inferior to that of her father (*Conv.* 213). Jonson had written *Hymenaei* in 1606 to celebrate Lady Frances's marriage to Robert Devereux, Earl of Essex. Immediately after the marriage, Essex left England for three years. While he was gone, Lady Frances and the king's new favorite, Robert Carr, Earl of Somerset, fell in love. Upon Essex's return, Lady Frances fled to her father's country estate, Audley End, but Essex found her, kidnapped her, and took her to his moated retreat, Chartley, in Staffordshire, where they lived for four years. But Lady Frances finally escaped and declared that the marriage had never been sexually consummated. On 25 September 1613, the king's commission of four bishops and six lawyers ruled that she was still, "to her shame and sorrow, *virgo intacta.*"[10]

To celebrate her subsequent marriage to Robert Carr on Boxing Day 1613, Jonson wrote two entertainments, *A Challenge at a Tilt* and *The Irish Masque,* and addressed a poem to Carr in which he prayed

> May she, whome thou for spouse, to day, dost take,
> Out–bee yt *Wife,* in worth, thy freind did make:
> And thou to her, that Husband, may exalt
> *Hymens* amends, to make it worth his fault.
> (*UV.* XVIII, ll. 12–14)

That *"Wife"* is Overbury himself, whose collection of misogynistic poems entitled The *Wife now the widdow* circulated in manuscript prior to its posthumous publication in 1614.

Lady Frances was a character in *The May Lord*, as were Overbury and Jonson—as Alken—himself (*Conv.* 395–97), and *The Sad Shepherd* is a version of that lost play, replete with thinly veiled references to the scandal that had centered around Lady Frances. She and her husband were convicted of murder. Lady Frances's serving woman, Anne Turner, who actually prepared and delivered the poisoned tarts to Overbury's cell, was executed. Lady Frances and Lord Somerset were imprisoned for a time and released. Somerset lived on quietly for many years, but Lady Frances was decried as a witch. Her story became another cautionary tale—like those of Eve, Bathsheba, Delilah, Ruth, and Tamar—which, as Mieke Bal has shown, "participates in the repression of women" (1987, 6). And this repression was specifically related—in every case—to the fear of women's sexuality. For example, the anonymous satirical ballad entitled *The Witch . . . made against the Lady Frances, Countess of Somerset* refers to her as one

> that could reek within the sheets of lust,
> And there be searched, yet pass without mistrust;
> She that could surfle up the ways of sin
> And make strait posterns where wide gates had been;
> Canidia now draws on.
> She that could cheat the matrimonial bed
> With a false–stamped, adultrate maidenhead
> And made the husband think those kisses chaste
> Which were stale pandars to his spouse's waste;
> Canidia now draws on.
>
> (in Broadbent 2.23)

In a patriarchal society, it seems, the charge of witchcraft inevitably involves men's fear of the uncontrolled sexuality of women.

The theme of women usurping men's roles is alluded to in *The Sad Shepherd* when Maid Marian, not Robin Hood, slays the deer and provides the feast. At least Maid Marian is seen in this role until Mother Maudlin, by assuming the shape of Marian, defrauds those "course rustick mouthes that cannot open" (1.7.6) of the venison she says is too good for them but which we, as the prospective audience, are made to feel is rightfully ours. So when Robin Hood meets the true Maid Marian who has been restored to her former self and repeats her disparaging words, we see how those familiar things fit into an ideological construct. This, in turn, enables us to be shocked when we recognize the class distinctions that inform our lives and the social barriers that reinforce those distinctions.

By calling attention to that part of society normally excluded from the stage except in roles of clowns or buffoons, *The Sad Shepherd* calls into question the rationalizations used by the ruling classes to represent their hegemonic power as part of a historic mission undertaken for the good of all. By presuming to unveil the social reality masked by ideology, this play allows us to create what Tony Bennett has described as "a kind of open, disengaged mental space within which a new attitude to reality might be produced." And by so doing, it "induce[s] a temporary suspension of ideology, a temporary release from its operations, which may give rise to a new form of attentiveness to and thoughtfulness about reality" (Bennett 1979, 126)—that is, a new form of attentiveness to *language* and to thoughtfulness about the discursive practices through which and by which notions about reality are produced and represented.

The question of who will feast on the venison epitomizes the larger question of who will inherit, who *deserves* to inherit, the future. The deception Mother Maudlin practices, and the manner in which we perceive it—at first as a change in Maid Marian's character and then, through Marian's eyes, as a trick practiced by Maudlin—further disrupts habitual perceptions. So when Maudlin enters dancing with joy over having been sent "so fat a Deere!" (2.6.6), we are momentarily bewildered. We do not know what to believe. Maudlin has been transformed from a sorrowful and brooding witch into a mirthful celebrant. Robin Hood judges her to be mad, but instead of reacting to this charge with hostility, Maudlin presents him with a gift of "A pott of Strawberries, gather'd i'the wood" (2.6.23) to show her good faith. Marian and Maudlin are, like the witches and queens of *The Masque of Queenes*, two aspects of the feminine forever competing for the phallus, Robin Hood himself, or his representation, the slain deer.

Maid Marian, while telling Mother Maudlin that she is mistaken to think she would willingly send the slain deer to her, refers to Robin Hood as "Red Deere," a hero who is "head still of the forrest feasts" (2.6.34). Marian and Maudlin, the provident and the perverted mother, two aspects of Artemis (Diana)—heavenly Phoebe and hellish Hecate—are not only fighting over who should provide the feast but also over who should inherit, possess, eat, and therefore make part of themselves the vitality Robin Hood represents. The deer is a scapegoat, a sacrificial animal sent out into the countryside where it was hunted and slain. And Marian/Maudlin is also a type of Agave, who, in a bacchanalian revel, attacks her son and slays him when he comes out of the city to spy on the women's ritual, a version of the sabbat. This revel was inspired by Dionysus, the hauntingly marginal Other-figure whose religion seeks to subvert the city-oriented religion by enjoining women to rebel against home and motherhood. An identity between Robin Hood and the slain deer is apparent in the next scene where Maudlin tells Marian, whom she now calls "a right free-hearted Ladie" (2.6.35), that she has divided the carcass "'mong my poore Neighbours/ To speake your Largesse" (2.6.37–38). But Marian is not fooled by Maudlin's cynical attempt to gain favor among the local peasants. She says she did not give the deer to Maudlin and tells her she has done wrong, for Marian knows how and where to give gifts and does not throw away her courtesies. Thinking she has caught Marian out, Maudlin immediately asks: "Count you this thrown away?" But Marian will have none of it. "What's ravish'd from mee," she replies, "I count it worse; as stolne" (2.6.42–43). This aspect of the play could easily be allegorized into an emblematic presentation of Maudlin as a representative of the joyless but shrewd Puritanism of the entrepreneurial classes, one who steals England's folk hero and his tradition of largesse. In this reading Marian would be seen as an aristocratic Artemis (Diana). Like the Countess of Rutland, who dismissed the witch Joan Flower, Marian offers open benevolence and *noblisse oblige* as she reclaims the vital heritage of folk culture for the aristocracy.

But such a schematic reading tends to flatten out and totalize the play's meaning; it marginalizes the way the play's emphasis on folk culture defamiliarizes courtly culture in the face of the new popular culture. For example, it minimizes the significance of thee fact that when Scathlock returns with the slain deer and Maudlin attempts to charm the carcass with a perverted prayer, another inversion of established beliefs is taking place. For instead of destroying the venison, the prayer awakens Amie from the trance she has been in since Karol kissed her and displaced her love of the natural world—of flowers, birds, and animals —with a love of man. She recalls his kiss, which, Maudlin reminds her, stung like a bee. Yet the remembrance of that pain is now sweet to her, sweeter even than the kisses she used to give her lambs, puppies, and the "daintie Roe-fawne I had" (2.6.107), but these kisses had "no such sting, or paine, as this" (2.6.110).

As in Marvell's "Nymph complaining for the death of her Faun," the conventions of pastoral keep innocent what readers may perceive as sexually suggestive. Amie's reluctant abandonment of undifferentiated love, like the nymph's extreme grief over the loss of her faun, transforms the innocent pastoral shepherdess into a woman. And in witnessing that transformation, we are awakened to the ideological function of pastoral. Therefore when we return to the scene of Amie's awakening, those aspects that previously seemed intrusive and digressive now appear central and essential. The love between Amie and Karol is emblematic of the central conflict between innocence and experience, the golden fictitious world of courtly pastoral and the sordid world of everyday reality. The play shows these supposed contraries to be but different aspects, different perceptions, of the ideas and behavior of the courtly elite. In this reading, Amie's fawn, like Maid Marian's slain deer, is symbolic of Robin Hood in his epiphany as the legendary Red Deer. This outlaw-hero stood in opposition to the supposedly refined tastes of the court and represented the only alternative to that classical culture that emerged from, and was dependent upon, ancient Greek and Latin texts—the folk culture with its roots in the oral traditions of the ephemeral "organic community."

Like Robin Hood, the slain deer represents both the vitality—the phallic function—and the vulnerability of folk culture. For that culture—like the "voice" of the poet in the text—is at once dead and alive. Like writing, which has overtaken orality; like the rise of print that has replaced manuscript culture; like the trade of playwright (a term Jonson invented but used only with contempt), which links writing and speech in an ambivalent manner; the slain deer provides food for the ritualistic feast. Mother Maudlin threatens to usurp the distribution of the slain deer; likewise, the phallic function Robin Hood represents is threatened in both the decaying aristocracy and the rising middle classes by what is perceived to be the castrating woman. Amie's lovesickness, then, focuses the key contradictions the play explores—the conflict between three forces: (1) a semipagan "organic community" rooted in "nature," that is, in the agrarian countryside represented by the folk culture figures of Maid Marian and Robin Hood, (2) a decaying courtly culture represented by the conventions of pastoral, and (3) the new popular culture with its ethic of possessive individualism.

The Sad Shepherd, then, does not look back nostalgically to the festive tradition of folk culture, nor does it lament its passing, as if the practices that comprise that culture somehow spoke their own authentic meaning voicing the "true" spirit of the people. It encapsulates the ideological crisis of Caroline England, but it also dramatizes the crisis of post-Cartesian subject formation. The phallic deer is hunted, killed, and slaughtered by Maid Marian under the eye of the raven, a form Mother Maudlin takes. And under Maudlin's spell, Maid Marian gives away the deer, which is identified with Robin Hood through his avatar Red Deer.

This triangular relationship is contrasted with the one whereby Amie's informed love for Karol is compared with her innocent love for her fawn. The anticipated feast, like the possession of the phallus itself, is forever delayed. In Robin Hood's bower, folk culture and courtly culture are rejoined in order to engender the Puritanical and repressive mores of the new popular culture that is busy being born.

5

The Great
Witch Hunt:
Hysteria vs. Reason

And as, in that rebellion 'gainst the gods,
MINERVA holding forth MEDUSA'S head,
One of the gyant brethren felt himselfe
Grow marble at the killing sight, and now,
Almost made stone, began t'inquire, what flint,
What rocke it was, that crept through all his limmes,
And, ere he could thinke more, was that he fear'd
So CATALINE, at the sight of *Rome* in us,
Became his tomb—
                                        Catiline (5.1.677–85)

I n *The Sad Shepherd* Jonson's persona, Alken, is locked
in battle with—and defines himself in relation to—a
representative of feminine sexuality, exemplified by the
witch Mother Maudlin. Through her ability to inhabit the
body of any living creature, she threatens to undermine
dramatic *mimesis* and, by implication, social stability itself. As a witch, a woman capable of deception, she renders appearances problematic and upsets the basis of social
communication. If we cannot depend upon the convention whereby we willingly suspend our disbelief, willingly
accept the fiction that the characters we see on the stage
—or in our mind's eye as we read—are who they pretend

134

to be, the bond between audience and player—as well as that between reader and author—is broken. We lose our willingness—indeed, our ability—to participate in the ritual of dramatic production, of *mimesis*.

This is what happens when Maid Marian appears in the opening of act one, scene seven. The original stage direction, as printed in the 1640 folio, simply says "To them *Marian.*" Does this mean that Maudlin should appear disguised as Marian? If this is the case, this would mean that the audience must be able to see through the disguise even though Robin Hood and his men cannot. This requires a more profound violation of *mimesis* than if the actor playing Maid Marian appears and acts in a way contrary to her previous—and therefore expected—behavior, because in that case the audience is not let in on the deception. But if Mother Maudlin *does* appear disguised as Maid Marian —if, in other words, we accept the fact that Maudlin has usurped Marian's identity—we must also believe that Robin Hood and his men cannot see what we can see, that the actor playing Maudlin is simply dressed as Marian. Following F. G. Waldron's 1783 edition, the Oxford editors opt for the mimetic violation and emend the folio to read "To them [*Maudlin, as*] *Marian.*"[1] In his 1816 edition William Gifford continues the scene but with the direction "*Re-enter Marian*" before Robin greets her. Gifford seems to have believed that the actor playing Marian must appear, not Maudlin dressed as Marian.

How this scene is read makes a great deal of difference, for by her possession of Maid Marian, Mother Maudlin does to Robin Hood what a play usually does to an audience: she persuades him to disbelieve his senses—"I dare not trust the faith of mine own senses" (1.7.14), Robin Hood had said earlier. Now he is asked to accept a palpable fiction, that Maudlin is Marian. But the audience "never absolutely accepts such fictions: we enjoy being brazenly lied to, we welcome for the sake of pleasure what we know to be untrue, but we withhold from the theater the simple assent that we grant to everyday reality"

(Greenblatt 1988, 119). Mother Maudlin's demonic possession of Maid Marian is responsibly marked out for the audience as a theatrical fraud designed to gull the unsuspecting. Alken, the old counsellor, notes that Maudlin has the ability to deceive the senses, but she cannot change her essential nature. Robin Hood reaffirms what the audience already knows when he expresses a desire to " . . . see her,/ Once more in *Marians* form!" for he is " . . . certaine/ Now, it was shee abus'd us" (2.6.124–27). Having warned us not to trust the evidence of our senses and having identified Maudlin as the source of evil deception, we now see the actors striving to exorcise that malignancy: "It was believ'd before, but now confirm'd," says Alken, "That wee have seen the Monster" (2.6.131–32).

Alken, a previously marginal figure, now moves into a central role; he says they must find some device to restrain the witch. Robin asks him to advise them. Alken replies that since the witch is a creature of melancholy, she will take the form of a hare.[2] But even though he knows the sport of witch-hunting, he is reluctant to assume a leadership role. He humbly asks permission to assist the huntsmen and fears he may be jeered or laughed at. He pleads that all his knowledge of how to hunt a witch is taken from books such as Tuberville's *Noble Arte of Venerie* and says that the only art he possesses that separates him from Robin and the others is that he, like the witch, knows how to read. Since he knows her shifts and haunts and all her wiles and turns, he promises to find her and " . . . lay/ My hand upon her; make her throw her skutt[3]/ Along her back . . ." (2.8.63–65), but he does not claim to be able to destroy her. There is, though, an implicit assumption that the simple exposure of the witch—a creature of the night—to the light of day will exorcise her power to subvert Maid Marian and Robin Hood's roles as providers for the common people. The act of exorcism, like that of demystification, holds out the (false) promise of coming to know pure truth uncontaminated by ideology.

A sympathetic understanding, a respectful affinity, exists between Alken and Mother Maudlin that is beyond the comprehension of the huntsmen, who merely wish to see the witch hanged. Alken, by contrast, has studied the same texts Maudlin has, and this intellectual bond sets them apart, distances them from the spontaneity of folk culture and distinguishes them both as marginal figures. No one in the play, including Alken, ever suggests that the witch is a criminal who should be reported to the ecclesiastical or legal authorities and made to stand trial. The very idea of ecclesiastical and/or legal restraint, of "placing" the "case" into the discourse of church and state, is never a possibility. The witch is hunted as an *animal*, not as a *criminal* or as an *outlaw*. Indeed, there is no unmediated voice of authority. *Everyone in the play is in some sense an outlaw.*

There is little wonder, then, that Alken sees Mother Maudlin as a dangerous adversary who threatens his position as sage counselor and moral arbiter, whereas Little John, Scarlet, Scathlock, and George a Greene see her only as a foul hag. To Robin Hood's men the hunt will be such "a stinking Chase!" that Scathlock would "rather ha' the hunting of her heyre" (2.8.72–73). The full meaning of this pun on the homonym air/hare/heir—which refers simultaneously to the witch's *odor du femme*, her transformation into the sexually ambivalent hare, and Maudlin's heir, either Lorel or, more likely, Douce—again draws attention to the inherent ambiguity of language, especially the ambiguity that arises when thoughtfully written words are spoken in a dramatic context in which they appear spontaneous. And this in turn gives rise to the opportunity for verbal irony. What is stated—the desire to capture the witch—is undercut by her suggestion that her distinctive feminine odor arouses Scathlock's sexual desire for her daughter. In addition, there is the play on the word "hare" that comes from its homonymic association with "whore," as it is in *Romeo and Juliet* (2.4.138–46).

But Alken, who was content at the end of the first act

"to await the issue" (1.7.37), is now eager to act, to con-
quer the witch who not only challenges his authority as
sage councelor, but who puts in question *before other men*
his very idea of himself. There is little wonder, then, that
Alken encourages Robin Hood's men to hunt the witch
down as they would an animal, to kill, cook, and eat her,
to incorporate her into themselves in order to stabilize
their gender identities as heterosexual men. The witch
must be exorcised in this way because she threatens the
stability of distinctions between masculinity and femininity, between outside and inside, physical self and mental
self, the body that suffers and the mind that creates.

And just as there is a parallel between Maid Marian's
hunt for the stag and Robin Hood and his men's hunt for
the witch, there is also a parallel between the aborted stag
feast and the aborted witch feast. Both of these parallels
echo the unresolved crisis of identity—of self—that crys-
tallized around key events of Jonson's life—his killing
of Gabriel Spencer, his conversion to Catholicism, his indictment for failure to take Anglican communion. The
obsessive dwelling upon eating, drinking, and festivity
throughout his works "plays out" Jonson's perpetual identity crisis, his inability to define himself without conflict
between trauma and fantasy. That is, Jonson appears to
be himself only when he represents himself—through
language—as an enigma. As he himself said, he was "Op-
pressed with fantasy, which hath over-mastered his reason" (*Conv.* 693–94).

This reading of the Jonsonian persona suggests that T.S.
Eliot's (re)construction of Jonson as a role model for the
modern(ist) intellectual/artist was indeed overdetermined. According to Eliot, in contrast to the more "popular,"
more "organic," more "spontaneous," and therefore more
"natural" genius of Shakespeare, Jonson was, like Eliot
himself, a conservative, Anglo-Catholic, monarchist. In
other words, Eliot saw Jonson as a model of what traditional intellectuals thought they were—or wanted to be
—or what radical intellectuals believed they were reacting against. Jonson was the strong poet of cultural elitism,

a heroic figure who fought a rear-guard action against the advancing vulgar tastes of popular culture.

The revival of academic interest in Jonson coincided with Eliot's identification of him as the chief opponent of a revolutionary Puritan ideology—represented by Eliot's view of Milton—that was culturally sterile, politically repressive, and philosophically deterministic. Jonson was thus seen as a valiant intellectual/artist caught between a decadent aristocracy whose patronage system was drying up and the emergent middle classes, whose ethos turned artistic production into commodity fetishism, thereby trivializing and debasing it. As one who strove—always unsuccessfully—to distance himself from all forms of authority, Jonson became the prototypical alienated intellectual/artist who strove—again always unsuccessfully—to achieve perfect autonomy.

I am not interested in determining the "accuracy" or "truth" of this view of Jonson, but I am troubled by the political implications of its unconscious—and therefore unself-reflexive—nostalgia. I am concerned about the way in which this view denies—or at least closes off—speculation about its own subject-position. Consider, for example, the assumptions behind Eliot's lament for the neglect of Jonson's masques: "our flaccid culture lets shows and literature fade, but prefers faded literature to faded shows. There are hundreds of people who have read *Comus* to ten who have read the *Masque of Blackness*" (1920a, 121–22). Such a bold comparison is based on the assumption that popular culture has lost its manly vitality precisely *because* it is no longer sufficiently courtly, no longer the preserve of a patriarchal elite whose claims to legitimacy are securely anchored in an organic concept of nature. That is, Eliot unself-reflexively—and nostalgically—laments the passing of a world where nature was seen as a maternal body that renewed itself in cycles.

In such a world, people living in organic communities saw their relationship to nature as reciprocal; they took food, shelter, and clothing from it, but in return they respected it and cared for it. When this concept of nature came to consciousness and was put into discourse—a sign that it was being called into question—men such as Richard Hooker tried to show how reason was based on a reading of nature as the model for society. In eight dense volumes of *The Laws of Ecclesiastical Polity*, the first four of which were published in 1593, Hooker explained how nature's great chain of being, which was immutable, reflected the social hierarchies, which were, it was hoped, thereby also made immutable. But, Hooker explained, even this orthodoxy could be violated. For nature was invested with supernatural phenomena such as magic, witchcraft, and other occult knowledges that the Church could not always control or channel through its hierarchies. Something of pagan animism clung to such beliefs.

As I noted in chapter one, in *The Discoverie of Witchcraft* Reginald Scot had tied such beliefs to Catholicism. He proclaimed that Robin Goodfellow was "a cousening idle frier, or some such roge, that wanted nothing either belonging to lecherie or knaverie" (1972, 48–49). In Jonson's masque *Love Restored*, Robin Goodfellow presents a lengthy history of his ill-fated attempts to retain his viability in the transition from a preliterate organic community of love to a literate culture corrupted by money. In the anonymous pamphlet *Robin Good-fellow, His Mad Pranks and Merry Jests* (1628), Goodfellow is an ithyphallic god of the witches.[4] Such examples of residual paganism indicate that Scot's efforts to rationalize the irrational were not totally successful, nor were they wholly supported by the authorities. King James was said to have ordered his book burnt.

James himself directed his *Daemonologie* against Scot, and after he assumed the British throne in 1603 he called a halt to witchcraft persecutions. Stuart Clark has observed that "there is little to suggest that [James] had any interest in propagating witchcraft beliefs in England at all." Like Pentheus in Euripides' *Bacchae*, James accepted "the argument *a posteriori* that witches are fun-loving hedonists because they attend spectacular orgies" (Clark 1977,

161) and sought to appropriate that Dionysianism. Thus, he could obviate the need to attack witches who, in some way, corresponded to the view of James's mother, Mary Queen of Scots, as a masterless, independent, autonomous woman—a phallic mother. As Christina Larner has noted, such a woman "is assertive; she does not require or give love (though she may enchant); she does not nurture men or children, nor care for the weak. She has the power of words—to defend herself or to curse" (1984, 84).

According to Clark, James's language "involved the classical 'similitudes' between monarchy, divine power, patriarchal authority and the role of the head of the human body." The head, the "upper phallus," was spiritualized and associated with God the Father and the body was associated with "feminine" earthly things such as childbearing. The pervasive "image of the upside-down world, in which the normal patterns of authority were inverted by, for instance, the rule of the body over the head or sons over fathers and subjects over princes" was one that always implied the fear of women ruling over men. What is more,

> The sexual exploits of witches also negated order, dethroning reason from a sovereign position on which not only individual well-being but social relations and political obligation were thought to depend. The surrender to passion was disorderly in more than the physical sense; kissing the Devil's arse ... was a highly charged symbolic act of political defiance.

Pierre de Lancre, a French judge of witchcraft trials whose works were eagerly read in England, thought witches "disordered the family by subverting patriarchal authority and destroying filial love." And since the head of state was father of his country, just as the head of the household was father of his children, men saw the *maleficium* of witches as an especially dangerous threat. "Above all," Clark observes, "the condition of a society dominated by women must have been seen as one of fundamental contrariety" (1977, 174–76).

In the opening scenes of the third act of *The Sad Shepherd*, Robin Goodfellow, also known as Puck-hairy, makes the connection between fathers, patriarchal order, and schoolmasters explicit:

> The Feind hath much to doe, that keepes a Schoole;
> Or is the Father of a familie;
> Or governes but a country Academie.
>
> (3.1.1–3)

But in the world of Robin Hood's bower, the nature of learning is totally ambiguous. In the family and school, patriarchal authority must labor hard "To watch all turnes, and cast how to prevent 'hem" (3.1.5). The witch, Puck explains, is deluded in her belief that she "growes high in evill" because of her own powers. According to Puck, "'tis I, her Divell,/ That both delude her, and must yet protect her" (3.1.7–8).

This complex relationship where Puck belongs to Maudlin, whom he misleads yet whom he must protect, parodies that between Prospero and Ariel in *The Tempest*. Puck announces that Maudlin simplisticly presumes that by changing her shape she will accomplish her purposes of subverting Marian and Robin's ideal relationship of mutual respect and sexual fulfillment, which is possible only within Sherwood Forest. But he knows better. Without his help Maudlin will be surprised and caught. He must therefore go dance about the forest and conduct himself "like a Goblin" (3.1.15) until he finds her. This "service" will prove his worth and his unexpected ability will make Maudlin accept him. As what? As

> When not expected of her; when the helpe
> Meetes the necessity, and both doe kisse,
> 'Tis call'd the timing of a dutie, this.
>
> (3.1.17–19)

In this curiously oblique manner, Puck expresses a desire to legitimize his relationship with Maudlin. He wishes to be recognized as her "help-meet," a term that usually

refers to a wife, and the words "necessity," "kiss," and
"dutie" form a series of oyxmoronic contradictions whereby what is involuntary—Puck's protection of Maudlin—
is called necessary, and what is voluntary—the reward of
a kiss—is, because of Puck's opportunistic timing, involuntary: "'Tis call'd . . . a dutie." Puck's speech, then, simultaneously puts forth even as it subverts its surface meaning. And this subversion suggests that the relationship
between other such hierarchical binaries may also be subverted. Once our attention has been drawn to such subversion, we see it everywhere.

For example, throughout the play personal identity as
an intrinsic autonomous selfhood is repeatedly put into
question. After Douce the Proud, still disguised in the
dress of Earine the Beautiful, allows herself to be caught
by the kind shepherd Karol, he sees that she is not Earine
who made "suite" against the feast planned by Marian and
Robin. The pun here—Earine's clothing and her objection
to the feast are both "suites"—epitomizes the kind of
"slippage" that forever defers any perfect correspondence
between a speech event or message (*parole*) and the system or code (*langue*). Karol points out that Earine would
have attended the feast as "an acceptable Guest" (3.2.6)
no matter what her dress or her objections may have
been; that is, as a representative of the feminine aspect of
the world of pastoral, the ideological mode of the court,
she would have been allowed to attend as an outsider, but
she was powerless to prevent the feast from taking place.
In this alternative culture of the folk, it is Marian and
Robin "Who are the Crowne, and Ghirland of the Wood"
(3.2.8), the central authority figures.

Douce responds as though Karol's words were a question. "I cannot tell," she replies. And for a moment we
are made to rethink the last line of Karol's speech. Did
he really ask who *are* the crown and garland of the
wood? Or did he not state that Marian and Robin are the
crown? But when Douce continues "my Mother gave it
mee,/ And bad mee weare it" (3.2.9–10), we are required

to rethink the previous lines and ask—wear what? the Crown?—and then answer, oh, no, she means Earine's dress, her suit. But no sooner has this thought flashed through our minds than Karol responds with another question: "Who, the wise good Woman? (3.2.10), which again confuses our expectations because we know that while Maudlin may be crafty and shrewd, she could only be called "wise" and "good" by someone who is misled, someone who is a stranger to the alternative world of Sherwood.

This confusion of identities continues as Aeglamour enters and Douce leaves. Aeglamour asks what Douce said. Karol answers "Who?" And Aeglamour replies that he thought he saw him talking to Earine "or her Ghost." But instead of waiting for an explanation he hurriedly asks if she identified who drowned her in the Trent or who raped her on "The rivers brim, the margin of the Flood?" (3.2.13–18). He is obsessed with the social implications of her alleged sexual violation:

> No ground is holie enough, (you know my meaning)
> Lust is committed in King Palaces,
> And yet their Majestie's not violated!
>
> (3.2.19–21)

Aeglamour's words invoke the theory of sanctuary, of a place separate from public or common ground that cannot be violated by the secular government or crown, only to question it. Aeglamour's words suggest that aristocratic men can sexually violate whomever they wish and not be charged with any crime. It may have been true that a woman monarch could have sex with whomever she wished—could be violated—and still be called the Virgin Queen, but that example merely demonstrated the difference between what was said and what was whispered. The idea of sanctuary—of a holy or sacred place—is heavily and deeply allusive. It is the virgule, the mark of difference, between public and private space, between material and spiritual values, and also between denotative and connotative meanings of the systems of signification at work in a particular society.

In *The Sad Shepherd*, Aeglamour's obsession with Earine's lost maidenhead, his blurred distinction between holy land and crown land, and his equally ambivalent remarks about the standard of sexual conduct "in Kings Palaces," highlight the difference between what was professed publicly as an ideal and what was whispered privately as gossip. The phallocentric ruling class, both nobles and gentry, enforced the conventional double standard whereby women were excluded from education and roles of responsibility—and therefore from official positions of power. These men viewed women as property over which they must enforce their patrimony by ensuring the virginity of a new wife and by demanding she not have sexual intercourse with other men after marriage. The further contradiction inherent in this social ethos was that women were also seen as sexually voracious and insatiable.

Aeglamour wants to recover a lost state of innocence, to postpone adulthood, marriage, and the responsibility of parenting. And since he expresses his own fears, not Earine's, his words take on the added complexity of displacement, in this case a sexual displacement that represents a desire to move back beyond the Fall. Aeglamour wishes to escape into an ideal land of childhood. There is also embedded within Aeglamour's concern for Earine's loss of virginity the patriarchal point of view that Earine's (assumed) rape was her "real" demise and her drowning merely anticlimactic, a sort of confirmation of her death as a socially useful and potentially productive mechanism. Having lost her maidenhead, she had lost the ability to ensure patrimony, that guarantee a man must have that the children who carry his name and inherit his property are truly his progeny.

Karol does not attempt to answer Aeglamour's questions regarding Earine's loss. Instead he undercuts the seriousness of the sad shepherd's speculations by letting us know that Aeglamour suffers from an unbalanced mind. "How sad," he says, "and wild his thoughts are!" And then he himself asks "gone?" (3.2.22) What are we to make of this inquiry? To what does it refer? Karol cannot be asking *if* Aeglamour's reason has left him, for he has just affirmed that it has. The question then must refer to Douce, disguised as Earine, who exited just as Aeglamour entered, or he may be referring to Earine herself, who is indeed gone. In the midst of this confusion over identity, Aeglamour contradicts himself and, following the dictates of conventional patriarchal morality, declares that Earine, as chaste as her name, which means maiden of the spring, "Dy'd undeflower'd: and now her sweet soule hovers,/ Here, in the Aire, above us" (3.2.24–25). Unable to cope with the idea of Earine being sexually violated by another man, Aeglamour, as Western metaphysics dictates, metamorphosizes her into pure spirit, thus denying altogether her physical—and therefore sexual—presence.

Earine is now, according to Aeglamour, in the Ptolemaic heavens. This astronomic reference associates the shepherd with scholasticism and further highlights his position as a representative of an anachronistic discourse. As a pastoral shepherd, he epitomizes the values of the court, but his excessive grief, like his complete acceptance of the Ptolemaic system, calls the relevance of that discourse into question. And, what is more, to confirm the apocalyptic implications of this decentering of the aristocratic ethos, the tearing away of Earine's maidenhead, the unveiling of her innermost self, heralds an age of "new concords!/ Delightfull harmonie!" which will "rock old Sages," (such as Alken?), who are entering their second childhood, "in the Cradle o'Speculation,/ And throw a silence upon all creatures!" (3.2.33–36)

To humor him, Karol compliments Aeglamour on this apocalyptic vision, this high rapture celebrating the cessation of speech, of *voice*, in the natural world:

> The loudest Seas, and most enraged Windes
> Shall lose their clangor; Tempest shall grow hoarse;

Loud Thunder dumbe; and every speece of storme
Laid in the lap of listning Nature, husht.

(3.2.38–41)

Silence, a key motif of the play, lies at the heart of the "issue" Robin earlier promised to pursue. And since, like Shakespeare, Jonson himself is silent about the ability of poetry, or prophecy, to bring paradise to earth, Aeglamour, like Lear, "questions a universe that never seems to answer back, and finds its essential meaning ... in silences, which is to suggest that even if the world is not meaningless its mysteries are beyond man's comprehension" (Wittreich 1984, 194).

But, unlike Lear, Aeglamour is merely sad, not tragic. As Joseph Wittreich has argued, Shakespeare's vision of the apocalypse differs from that of his contemporaries in that "within the sardonic or false apocalypse of the play ... lies a prospect for apocalypse in the future, not perhaps in a future eternity but within future history and to be effected not by John of Patmos's God but by man himself" (1984, 195). By emphasizing the patriarchal and elitist aspects of the apocalyptic vision and by locating such a vision in the context of the construction, appropriation, and marginalization of folk culture, this reading of *The Sad Shepherd* demystifies that vision and places the responsibility for shaping the future on the shoulders of *all* men and women, not just the *men* of a particular class. To recapture the prospect for a new Golden Age, we need to do more than divorce the apocalyptic vision from its theological context; it is not simply a matter of humanizing such a vision, nor is it a question of further secularizing it. Apocalypticism has been unveiled; its phallocentrism, its hope of mastering nature and subordinating others as a means of allaying the fear of castration has been discredited.

Whatever sorrow we might feel for Aeglamour is rendered ambivalent by his "unmanly" self-pity and distracted grief. But the dialogic nature of the play's language inhibits such a simple and simpleminded reading.

Aeglamour's denial of nature's personal presence, his pressing imposition of selfhood as the embodiment of God as the logos, as the living human *voice*, is distanced through his unmanly sorrow. This detaches Aeglamour from culpability. Aeglamour may therefore utter aloud that which more rational, less distracted, and therefore more socially conventional characters cannot. His repeated references to Earine's virginity also point up the contrast between folk and courtly views of women. Earine, the courtly woman, is a vulnerable piece of sexual property; but Maid Marian/Mother Maudlin, the Janus-faced carnivalized woman of folk culture, is masterless, in charge of her own sexuality.

As we have seen, Lady Frances Howard's story did more than upset conventional pieties. It exposed the vulnerability of patriarchy, and since Overbury was a leader of the decidedly phallocratic inner court circle, his murder became a focal point for what David Underdown has called "The flood of Jacobean antifeminist literature and the concurrent public obsession with scolding, domineering, and unfaithful wives." This, in turn, reinforced "widespread fears that in familial as well as in community relations the world was badly out of joint" (1985, 38). The misogynist tradition that Chaucer's Wife of Bath inveighs against, which was strengthened during Elizabeth's reign and which James was seen to encourage, led dramatists such as John Marston and Thomas Middleton to depict female independence as a form of sexual inversion that threatened the social order.

The court of King James was then—and is still—often represented as carnivalesque, but attitudes toward this representation varied then as they still do now. The conservative view was, and is that the spectacles of the Jacobean court—both those, such as Jonson's masques, which were under artistic control and those, such as the scandal of Lady Frances, which were were under legal control— were necessary for the support of monarchy. Such spectacle functions as a kind of reverse scapegoatism. Royals are "allowed" to do these things so "we" do not need to. Those who take this view often also excuse carnival-esque behavior by lower-class people, often invoking the functionalist or safety valve hypothesis, and dismiss the transgressive potential of such behavior. But there are also those who condemn Jacobean excess outright as morally indefensible. Those who take this view usually distinguish between different kinds of excess, some—such as public shows—being acceptable, while others, of a sex-ual nature, are condemned. There is also the historicist view that says the excesses of the Jacobean court are un-derstandable in the context of the time but are unac-ceptable now, usually because such practices are seen to be misogynistic and supportive of patriarchy.

If we consider the conjunction of witchcraft and hys-teria in light of Foucault's work on "discursive forma-tions" and Michel Pecheux's work on "interdiscourse," we see that allegations of witchcraft, such as those directed against Lady Frances, may reflect the ways in which wo-men's rebellion against patriarchy was—and still is—demarcated and circumscribed, cut-off, in effect, from civilized, rational, discourse.[5] The first English work on hysteria, *A Brief Discourse of a Disease Called the Suf-focation of the Mother*,[6] was published in 1603, the year of King James's accession. Its author, Edward Jorden (or Jordan) had advised James to denounce the persecution of witches. James Hillman has called Jorden's book "a water-shed, separating the ancient superstition called possession from the modern superstition called hysteria." Hillman gives Jorden's book high praise because it moved the mat-ter of hysteria "from an irrational religious problem to one of secular explanation. But," Hillman notes, "the sinister misogynist implications remain. The witch is now a poor patient—not evil, but sick" (1972, 254).[7]

Jorden's efforts to rationalize and control the challenges to patriarchy that witchcraft represented was no more successful than Scot's efforts were a century earlier. Hey-wood and Brome's *Late Lancashire Witches* exemplifies how witchcraft retained its potential to subvert patriarchal order and undermine conventional assumptions about the proper role of women in a society where acquisitiveness and individualism were becoming dominant values. The play satirizes the government's liberal policies toward witchcraft prosecutions by poignantly presenting the case of a sceptic, Mr. Generous, who is finally convinced that his loving and attentive wife is a witch. R. Trevor Davies has observed that "the supreme object" of the play "must have been to intensify public feeling against witches and to confound sceptics by following as closely as possible the evidence given at the trial at Lancaster" (1972, 114). Mr. Generous's married life is one of exceptional happiness and affection, but the evidence of his wife's witchcraft mounts to where, in the end, he cheerfully hands her over to the gallows. As old Seely notes near the end:

> We all have had our errors, and as plainly/ It now appearse, our judgments, yea our reason/ Was poyson'd by some violent infection,/ Quite contrary to Nature. (1634, 254)

Contemporary reports of the famous case of witchcraft and possession at Loudon, which occurred shortly after Heywood and Brome's play was first staged, performed a similar function. The entire scenerio was luridly reported in England by Walter Montague, who converted to Catholicism after witnessing the exorcism of the nuns (K. Thomas, 1971, 492). As Underdown has noted, "The endless reiteration" of the dangers wrought upon the social fabric by rebellious women "would have been unnecessary if there had not been uneasy feelings" about them (1985, 39).

In *The Sad Shepherd*, as we have seen, Mother Maudlin, "The Envious . . . Witch of Paplewick," attempts to destroy the harmonious relationship between Robin Hood, Maid Marian, and other inhabitants of Sherwood Forest. Her indeterminate identity causes contradictions between the animistic participatory consciousness associated with folk culture and the new rationalist Cartesian discourses which maintained that there were no such things as witches, demonically possessed women, and that women who acted belligerently, who were unsubordinated to men, were suffering from natural causes. Supposed witches, such as Mother Joan Flower (the model for Mother Maudlin) and Lady Frances Howard (the model for Maid Marian) were suffering from hysteria. They were physically ill.

The ways in which Mother Maudlin confuses the question of identity, of stability of character, dramatizes the confusion that resulted from these conflicting discourses. She upsets everyone's knowledge of who they are and who they appear to be to others. After Aeglamour departs, Clarion asks Lionel if it was not the Sad Shepherd they just saw leaving. "Yes, I ghesse it was," Lionel responds. "Who was that left you, *Karol* ?he asks. To which Karol responds, "The lost man!/ Whom, wee shall never see himselfe againe;/ Or ours, I feare!" (3.3.2–5) Karol's contorted syntax draws attention to the fact that Aeglamour's sadness over the loss of Earine has caused him to lose his reason, his identity. He is now another person, not the Aeglamour that they once knew, and, Karol fears, such a loss of identity is infectious. If they no longer know who Aeglamour is, they each lose a bit of their own identity since identity is constituted in relationship to others.

But despite his loss, Aeglamour maintains what he believes to be a "natural," rebellious, "unmanly"—and therefore feminine identity:

> . . . He starts away from hand, so,
> And all the touches, or soft stroke of reason,
> Yee can applie! No Colt is so unbroken!
> Or hawke yet halfe so haggard, or unmann'd!
>
> (3.3.5–8)

Karol is especially wary of Aeglamour's spiritualization of Earine, his metaphysical transformation of her into "a Sphere amid the seven" to which Aeglamour "reades a Musique-Lecture" and imagines that the planets themselves hear him (3.3.12–14). To Karol, a conventional pastoral shepherd, this inversion of the idea that one may hear the music of the Pythagorean spheres if one is versed in alchemical and Rosicrucian lore is an unsettling delusion of grandeur, a sure sign of dementia. If Aeglamour had simply claimed to be able to hear the music of the spheres, Karol might view him as a prophet, a visionary poet in touch with the godhead. But this identification is forestalled by Aeglamour's claim, through Karol, that he is able to teach the planets how to sing. As I noted in chapter four, such outlandish declarations place Aeglamour in the same category as mad Empedocles. Self-delusion, then, is the ultimate loss of identity because it is the ultimate withdrawal from society, from commerce with others, or with the Other.

The remaining lines of the play are replete with ambiguities and confusions. Just as we are being lead to take Aeglamour's delusion seriously, Clarion assures us that his is only "a strayn'd, but innocent phant'sie!" (3.3.15) At this point the effort to determine everyone's "true" identity becomes even more intense. In order to determine whether Karol truly loves his sister Amie, Lionel stares at Karol so hard that Karol is frightened. Lionel wishes he could see whether Cupid has lodged an arrow in Karol's breast as he has in his sister's. As they are about to leave to visit the lovesick Amie, Maudlin, disguised as Marian, enters with her daughter Douce.[8]

As in act 1, scene 7, we have a confusion of identity between Maid Marian and Mother Maudlin that forces us to distance ourselves from the characters and actions we are witnessing. Maudlin, as Marian, tells Lionel and Karol that she has cured Amie of her lovesickness with the help of "Mother/ *Maudlin*, the cunning Woman" (3.4.22–23). And she assures them that "the skill of that wise woeman/ And her great charitie of doeing good" has "wrought effects, beyond beliefe" (3.4.31–32, 34). Lionel is skeptical;

he finds it "strange, that any art should so helpe nature/ In her extremes" (3.4.37–38). But Karol tells him that art "appeares most reall/ When th'other is deficient" (3.4.38–39). The dense ambiguities here point to a crisis of definition that has gone past the point of mere personal identity. The most dependable binary of Renaissance humanism has broken down, and we are presented with a world in which we can no longer tell the difference between appearance and reality, art and nature.

The mimetic deception, the willing suspension of disbelief "previously" confined to the stageplay world, has "now," in the written text, become universal, and this means that we no longer have a dependable reality we can use to measure fantasy. In the Alice-in-Wonderland world of textuality, all metaphors are literalized. The demarcations between make believe and truth are rendered obsolete. What had previously been confined to the world of the stage—the conscious acceptance of deception—has now spread to society at large. In *The Staple of News*, the fate of Pocahantas exemplifies how contact with dissolute Europeans corrupts the aristocrats of nature (2.5.121–24; 2.Inter.40–45); in *The Sad Shepherd*, the confusion that abounds in the marginalized organic community dramatizes a similar corruption.

The Sad Shepherd is set in the landscape surrounding Belvoir Castle, country estate of the Manners family, the Earls and Countesses of Rutland. King James visited the estate on his way to assume the throne in 1603, and in 1612 Prince Henry rode 96 miles in two days to join his father there. James visited the estate again in 1614, in 1617, and in 1621 he came there to see *The Gypsies Metamorphos'd*. These events, together with the scandal involving Lady Frances Howard, are, as we have seen, part of the text of the play. Such a profusion of references undermines the humanist concept that everyone must fashion a stable, fixed identity. This theme becomes overt when Robin Hood enters and asks why everyone is standing around talking when innocent Amie needs help.

Lionel tells him that "your *Marian*" has told them that Amie has recovered. "My *Marian*?" Robin replies. Surely the figure he *sees* is not the Marian he has known, not the Diana-figure who hunted and slayed the deer and delivered it to him. When she hears Robin Hood' voice, Maudlin-as-Marian says "Robinhood? Is hee here?" (3.4. 42–44) Maudlin's *voice*, that most determining of all presences, gives her away, for after he hears Maudlin's voice Robin *knows* this is not "his" Marian, and this awareness allows him to treat this witch as a rebellious woman whose sexuality must be contained within the boundaries of patriarchal society. Maudlin at once realizes this and starts to run away; Robin shouts "Stay!" and pursues her.

As in Greek tragedy, violence that takes place offstage is all the more disturbing because what we imagine to happen offstage is more "real" than anything that could be shown onstage. Maudlin's screams enable us to vivify the violation that takes place out of sight: "Helpe, murder, helpe," she cries. "You will not rob me, Out-law? Theife, restore/ My belt that yee have broken!" (3.4.45–47) Now of course Robin Hood is indeed an outlaw, one who lives outside the legal parameters of patriarchal society, but Maudlin's attempt to disguise herself as Marian, and Robin's ability to detect, by hearing her voice rather than by seeing her, that this is not the real Marian, inverts these parameters of behavior. The privileging of speech over sight inverts the normative sensory priority.

Robin's "rape" of the witch, who represents the malevolent aspect of the feminine Other, breaks the demonic possession that threatened the hegemony of patriarchy. He humiliates the rebellious woman and subordinates her. Like a proper gentleman, like Lord Buckingham, like Lorel the Rude, Robin here becomes the guardian of patriarchy. The violence against Mother Maudlin is legitimate because it reinscribes patriarchy. It offsets the (suspected) rape of Earine. Robin returns with the broken enchanted belt, emblem of magic, witchcraft, of women's mysteries,

and of the hymen that ensures female chastity and therefore a woman's value as marketable property, and Mother
Maudlin returns "in her own shape." Robin says he will
give back the now broken belt if Mother Maudlin will
"come neere" (3.4.47). But she knows that if she does he
will capture her. She therefore declines the offer to re-
trieve the shattered symbol of her power.

At this moment, when he is in fact *called* an outlaw,
Robin Hood sheds his Dionysian identity and aligns himself with patriarchy. In the same manner that Perseus
holds aloft the head of the Gorgon Medusa in *The Masque
of Queenes*—and Macduff holds aloft the severed head of
Macbeth (5.8.64)[9]—Robin Hood holds the witch's broken
belt and voices his triumph:

> Was this the charmed circle?
> The Copy that so couzen'd, and deceiv'd us?[10]
> I'le carry hence the trophie of your spoiles.
> My men shall hunt you too upon the start,
> And course you soundly.
>
> (3.4.48–52)

But Robin Hood's sudden violent assertion of masculine
dominance is short-lived, for the witch challenges the
sexual basis of the ideology of the ruling class with her
immediate announcement that if Robin's men continue
to hunt her down she will send them home without
their legs or arms. As a castrating phallic mother she will
"free" them from nature, from instinctive behavior, and
initiate them into the symbolic order, into culture. In
that symbolic order, they will have to use language to
define themselves in relation to one another, that is, in relation to an Other.[11]

According to the argument of the third act of *The Sad
Shepherd*, after Robin Hood seizes Mother Maudlin's
magic belt, her son Lorel starts to rape Earine, but he is
prevented by the approach of Clarion and Aeglamour. As
they come near, they hear Earine singing from inside the
tree. Believing her voice to be that of an angel, Aeglamour

refuses to try to free her, but Clarion sees her hand and begins to court it. Maudlin sends a mist to confuse him, and, cursing the loss of her magic belt, she slinks off to her dell where she is found by Alken and the huntsmen "with her Spindle, Threds, and Images" (l. 56). The huntsmen wish to capture her, but Alken persuades them to let her begin her charms. As a result, "shee escapeth them all, by the helpe and delusions of *Puck*" (ll. 60–61).

The phallic mother, the castrating witch, embodies the ambivalent promise of future joy, of pleasure, of love, that is endlessly deferred and therefore never kept. In addition, as the tabooed "Mother" Maudlin (as opposed to the chaste—but sexually available—"Maid" Marian), the witch also foregrounds the incest motif, which is latent in Robin Hood's relationship with Maid Marian. This female figure's unbridled sexuality threatens the rights of patriarchy, a man's need to know who his children are—and who may therefore legitimately inherit his name and estate—which justifies his right to insure that a woman does not have sexual relations with other men.

Up until the point of his violent attack on Mother Maudlin, Robin Hood is a passive hero. Just as he neither hunts nor kills the deer, he neither initiates lovemaking with Maid Marian nor leads the hunt for the witch. This passivity is a function of his estrangement from patriarchal society and from the humanist model of self-fashioning. Robin Hood has no job, ownes no shares in a stock company, has no money invested in any venture, has title over no landed estate, and has no heirs to inherit his patrimony. But when Robin Hood "rapes" Mother Maudlin, he asserts the fact that he can rejoin patriarchal society at any time he chooses. Within Sherwood Forest he lives by his own wiles and by the largesse of his (male) friends and the good will that he shares with other men who do not attempt to assert rights of ownership over nature. But his monogamous relationship with Maid Marian—and his violation of Mother Maudlin—suggest that while he only partially shares the attitudes and values that support a patriarchal-capitalist society, his position is forever ambivalent. Like Dionysus, he blurs carefully defined boundaries and is always positioned in "an in-between state where fluidity challenges stability, where fusion replaces boundary" (Segal 1982, 13).

We cannot be sure of anything within the fragile world of Robin Hood's bower, but this uncertainty suggests that the alternative world of knowledge represented in official discourse by the occult, by alchemy and witch-craft—a world about which Jonson had gone to great lengths to inform himself—cannot be dismissed with the "enlightened" rationalistic assumption that now we know better. Indeed, that is precisely the point that Reginald Scot does not "get" in his effort to explain away witch-craft as merely "a cousening art, wherin the name of God is abused, prophaned and blasphamed, and his power attributed to a vile creature" (1972, 274).[12] Indeed, it is precisely the problematic state of witchcraft that *The Masque of Queenes* and *The Sad Shepherd* dramatize.

In *The Sad Shepherd* the legend of Robin Hood, iden-tified with folk culture, remote woodlands, and outlawry, intrudes upon and subverts courtly pastoral conventions. In this perspective, witchcraft, which is *part of* that same folk culture from which the legends of Maid Marian and Robin Hood spring, may now be seen as a transgressive alternative *within* popular culture. Witchcraft is thus "a lively reaction of a peasant consciousness disillusioned with the ideologies of urban origin" (Le Roy Ladurie 1974, 207). The operative phrase here is "lively reàction," which tends to romanticize superstition and obscurantism. Witchcraft, like hysteria, was not simply—or at least not only—a fiction created by men who wished to persecute masterless young women or eccentric old ones, nor was it merely an attempt by authorities to justify suppression of unruly peasants. It was also, as Le Roy Ladurie notes, "a lively reaction," an attempt on the part of women and peasants to resist concrete and specific threats to their autonomy and their culture. These threats manifested themselves in a concentrated effort to enclose common arable land. The peasant uprisings that occurred repeatedly from 1381 to 1495 suggest that peasants saw enclosures as an attempt to take away land they had been free to use for as long as any of them could remember. Underdown reports that as late as 1612 protesters against enclosures were called "Robin Hoods" (1985, 110).

Witchcraft arose out of this situation. As P. T. W. Baxter's research in East African communities has shown, witchcraft accusations are "most frequent where cultivation is essential to subsistence and rights over land have economic importance" (1972, 171; quoted in Rigby 1985, 100). In pastoral societies, where the grazing of livestock is predominant, witchcraft accusations are negligible, but in societies where land cultivation is predominant, people see themselves in competition for limited resources " 'so that one man's gain inevitably involves another man's loss, and a type of occult mercantilism prevails.' Witchcraft and sorcery are used to 'steal' fertility or plants from neighbours' fields into one's own" (Baxter, 1972, 172; quoted in Rigby 1985, 100).

Part of the mythology of Western civilization is that in an oral pastoral society, an "organic community," labor is more cooperative than in a literate agricultural society. Land is controlled communally in both cases, but in an agricultural society, humans appropriate nature (i.e., land) through natural rights vested in individuals, so the objectification of nature is rationalized through the intimidating exclusivity, fixity, and "legitimacy" of writing, as a "polarization . . . of the subject (individual cultivator) and object (land/nature)" (Rigby 1985, 101). In addition, the discourse that produces and is produced by this polarization encourages the production of a subjectivity that separates things that can be categorized as cultural—"artificial" —from those that are "natural," and the discourse calls attention to this separation.

The Second Coming:
A Popular Patriarchal Voice

Throwe, Holye Virgin, then
  Thie Chrystall sheild
About this Isle, and Charm the rounde, as when
  Thou mad'st in open ffield
The Rebell Gyante stoope, and Gorgon Envye yield—
  Ode: (*UV.* XLVIII, ll. 37–41)

How, then, can we help displace the patriarchal ethos represented—and reinscribed—by Perseus's beheading of Medusa and Robin Hood's violation of Mother Maudlin? To address this question we must look at the myths of origin that underlie popular culture, for it is through these myths that patriarchy is legitimized. The myth of origin most often used in this way posits an originary festival. As Derrida has pointed out, Rousseau himself held that "The origin of . . . society is not a contract . . . . It is a *festival* [*fete*] (1977, 262). And as Hegel confirmed in *The Phenomenology of Spirit,* "The True is . . . the Bacchanalian revel in which no member is not drunk" (1977, par. 47). A century later Freud located the incest taboo, and hence the Oedipus complex, in the guilt that resulted from a primal patricidal scene. Men's desire to assuage guilt for having murdered the father and for having had sexual relations with mothers, aunts, and sisters,

159

led to the creation of the totem feast—"mankind's earliest festival"—in which the murder of the father was reenacted by the sacrifice of scapegoat accompanied by triumphant rejoicing and wild dancing. Such a festival, Freud explained,

> is a permitted, or rather an obligatory, excess, a solemn breach of a prohibition. It is not that men commit the excesses because they are feeling happy as a result of some injunction they have received. It is rather that excess is of the essence of a festival; the festive feeling is produced by the liberty to do what is as a rule prohibited. (1955g, 140)

Freud said that Greek tragedy reinscribed this obligatory excess; the sufferings of the divine goat, Dionysus, expatiated for the guilt of patricide and incest, thus maintaining the cohesiveness of the community under a dispersed, yet still patriarchal, authority. Christianity adapted this idea from the Orphic doctrine of original sin that said humans "were descended from the Titans, who had killed the young Dionysus-Zagreus and had torn him to pieces." But since "in the Christian myth the original sin was one against God the Father," in Christian doctrine men acknowledged their guilt of murdering their father and having sex with their female relatives by sacrificing one of their sons. "Atonement with the father was all the more complete since the sacrifice was accompanied by a total renunciation of the women on whose account the rebellion against the father was started" (1955g, 154).

Thus the women who had been made accessible by the murder of the father saw the possibility of a maenadic identity as a (potential) rebellion against masculine dominance. As Charles Segal has explained:

> Dionysus' cult gives to women a power and an importance that were denied them . . . . Yet it does so in a complex and ambiguous way. Dionysus releases the emotional violence associated with women and gives it a formalized place in ritual, a ritual not in the polis but in the wild . . . . Dionysus is felt to have a special affinity with women not only

because he symbolizes the repressed emotionality associated with the female but also because he himself spans male and female (1982, 159).

Catherine Clément and Carlo Ginzburg have both suggested that this maenadic identity shows that the excess of festivity is never effectively inscribed within the patriarchal ethos. The witches sabbat—the symbolic representation of the return of the repressed—constantly challenges the patriarchal ethos by acknowledging what is called madness, anomality, and perversion.[1] These theorizations, in turn, suggest that changes in language usage in discourse, may indicate that the patriarchal ethos is being displaced.[2]

As we have seen, the language that Ben Jonson used in his poems, plays, and masques is often laden with ambivalence, with indications that there is something unarticulated, unexposed, with regard to gender roles. There is no easy answer to the question of whether or not these plays and masques reinscribe the patriarchal ethos or undermine it. Or, rather, the easy answer is that they do both. The women to whom Jonson dedicated many of his plays and masques, and from whom he received much of his patronage and inspiration, were close to, but displaced from, the centers of power. They were a form of property, not property holders.[3] Defenders of the humanist tradition as well as feminists who are antagonistic to that tradition agree on this point. According to Graham Parry,

> Jonson's serious appraisal of feminine lives represented a new development in English letters: his poems to the great ladies of his time are contributions to a humanist view of society in which men and women move on equal terms, in which character, although conditioned by ancestry and breeding, is essentially a conscious creation of liberal spirit." (1985, 172–73)

And according to Kathleen McLuskie, because of his "apparently clear-eyed demystification of the 'real' relations between men and women, the true nature of the marriage market, and the pathetic emptiness of male sexual fantasy and the focus of power within sexual relations . . . Jonson [is] an attractive writer for feminists" (1989, 191).[4] Indeed, Jonson's deep and lasting friendships with these women is an essential part of the the author-function's marginality, its potential for transgression.

Aphra Behn, the first woman to earn her living by producing texts for popular cultural consumption, was also the first to point out that Jonson's ability to exploit the humanist tradition of classical republicanism[5] depended on the construction of a gendered subjectivity. "For waving the examination, why women having equal education with men, were not as capable of knowledge, of whatever sort, as well as they," she wrote,

> I'll only say . . . that Plays have no great room for that which is mens great advantage over women, that is Learning: We all well know that the immortal *Shakespears* Playes (who was not guilty of much more of this than often falls to womens share) have better pleas'd the World than *Johnsons* works, . . . [but] I have seen a man the most severe of *Johnsons* Sect, sit with his Hat remov'd less than a hairs breath from one sullen posture for almost three hours at the Alchymist; who at the excellent Play of *Harry* the Fourth . . . hath very hardly kept his Doublet whole; but affectation hath always had a greater share both in the actions and discourse of men than truth and judgement have (H&S 11.534).

Behn saw that the ability to be convinced of an author's *presence*, to feel his or her existence as a living being behind the words on the page, was dependent upon our perception of a self that had undergone a separation from an imagined originary wholeness. And Johnson's plays evoked this perception more convincingly than Shakespeare's. Plays by the unlearned—and therefore "feminine" —Shakespeare made men uncomfortable.

Jonson's precocity, if that is what it is, in this matter may be attributed to the fact that his literary father, Horace, showed him how to create an apparently timeless presence through writing. And this timeless presence was a decidedly masculine one—one which, as Jonson documented in *The Masque of Queenes*, defined itself in opposition to a malevolent notion of femininity, to witches. This masculine consciousness, which became known as Cartesian subjectivity, was defined in opposition to a lost tribal unity. The voice-in-the-text, the secularized transposition of the Parousia, is Jonson's most enduring accomplishment. And as the founder of this author-function, Jonson's legacy was thoroughly ambivalent. The next generation of poets—the sons of Ben—were split in their view of their father figure. On one hand, there were those loyal supporters of the court—Sidney Godolphin, Henry King, Thomas May, George Fortesque, William Habington, Edmund Waller, William Cartwright, Owen Felltham, among others—who, in *Jonsonus Virbius: or, The Memorie of Ben Johnson*, appropriated the Jonsonian presence. They divested this presence of its hostility to the Caroline court and made it palatable by praising it as the face of a venerable monument, by seeing Jonson as a cantankerous old curmudgeon whose charm belied his rocky facade. In this way they diffused any threat that presence may have posed *to* themselves, that is, to their representation of themselves to themselves and to others who were in basic accord with the ideology of the Caroline court. Jonson's immodest rage exposed their subservience to an outmoded system of patronage; therefore, they had to see him as a petulant, laughable figure whose harsh words, like his Horatian persona, were *merely* a mask.

There were others, however, who did not contribute to the official commemorative volume and who saw Jonson somewhat differently. Robert Herrick, who prayed for "Saint Ben' to guide him "For old *Religions* sake" (H–604), withdrew into the Devonshire countryside, into the vanishing world of the folk festivals, whose carnivalesque atmosphere was imbued with what Patrick Cruttwell has called "a tinge of more solemn feeling, relic of the religion they had sprung from" (159). In his epitaph for Jonson,

Herrick simply says that though Jonson "lyes . . . with the rest/ Of the Poets," he is "the Best" (H–910). There is no indication of time, no past tense that would call attention to Jonson's death. Instead, by questioning the reader in the past perfect conditional—"wo'dst thou more have known?"—the poem introduces an ambiguity of time on the side of the reader. This implies that we *should* have known more about Jonson, that there *was* more that we should have bothered to find out about him, *before* he died.

Having planted this implied chastisement in our minds, the poem then tells us that it is not too late to find out about Jonson. If we "Aske his Story, not this Stone,/ That will speake what this can't tell/ Of his glory." This emphasis on the spoken voice is in the Ode "for," not "to," Jonson (H–911), which invokes Jonson's presence with a deliberately contradictory plea for him to

> Say how, or when
> Shall we thy Guests
> Meet at those *Lyrick* Feasts,
>   Made at the *Sun*,
> The *Dog*, the triple *Tunne*?
>
> (ll. 2–6)

By calling for the dead poet to speak, the speaker of this poem fondly recalls times he spent with Jonson when they became "nobly wild, not mad" (l. 7); in this festive atmosphere, Jonson's voice was more nourishing than his "meate" or his "frolick wine" (l. 10). By reading Jonson's poems, by re-creating his presence, his voice, we too can be nourished. The speaker's version of *"Ben"* will thus return. But the poem undermines the simplicity of this Parousia, this facile Second Coming; the repetition of the word "or" introduces the two alternatives: "Or come agen:/ Or send to us" (ll. 12–13). This causes us to doubt the idea that by reading Jonson's verse we will experience his original presence and also makes us skeptical about the proposition that follows: that, through his "wits great overplus" (l. 14), Jonson can "teach us yet/

Wisely to husband" that wit, "that Tallent" (ll. 15–17), which, as the parable teaches—Matt. 25.14–30—is death to hide. That Jonson would teach anyone *not* to spend anything, either talent or money—the two are the same in the Bible—raises the vexing question of his alleged anality, his notorious profligacy, and his frequent equation of reading and writing with feeding and festivity. No less ambiguous are the poem's apocalyptic final lines, which warn that once Jonson's wit has been used up and "brought to an end/ . . . the world sho'd have no more" (ll. 19–20).

The poem's second stanza, then, contradicts the conventional notion, alluded to in the first stanza, that we can reproduce an author's presence simply by reading his poems. This gap and discontinuity between the arguments of the two stanzas manifests the hiatus between, on the one hand, the logical notion of the cultural mainstream that a poem re-presents—offers the opportunity to re-create, re-produce—the presence, the voice, of the poet and the experience the poem describes, and, on the other hand, the culturally marginal rhetorical idea that no such thing is possible, that there is no such thing as pure repetition, that time dictates that there must always be a separation, a difference between impulse and idea, between idea and expression, between signifier and signified. And this gap, this radical discontinuity, validates the notion of the apocalypse—that a new beginning, a new identity, a new world, is possible.

In the very act of reaffirming Jonson's presence, the poem calls into question the possibility that the Jonsonian wit will go on forever. There was a time, the poem reminds us, when Jonson's wit did not exist, and there will be such a time again. Herrick also lamented that on the London stage after Jonson's death

> . . . men did strut, and stride, and stare, not act.
> Then temper flew from words; and men did squeake,
> Looke red, and blow, and bluster, but not speake:
> (H-382, ll. 6–8)

This seemingly small, personal, and exquisitely private contemplation of the end of Jonson's "voice" is, in its way, a corresponding interiorization of a more overtly political notion of apocalypse that informed the leaders of the Parliamentary Army. These leaders ejected Herrick and other clergymen who refused to literalize apocalyptic metaphors and chastize their slothful parishoners for maypole and morris dancing, participation in wakes, tilting matches, shearing feasts, harvest homes, wassails, mummeries and Christmas revels, as well as for belief in fairy lore, witchcraft, and sympatheic magic. Robert B. Hinman has observed that "Herrick writes as though he were a primitive" (1970, 162). That "as though" is a key to Herrick's ability to make us feel we are in touch with a world behind—in both a historical as well as a metaphysical sense—the world of fallen nature and Baconian empirical science that replaced the world of oral presence in which God spoke to poets and poets spoke to men.

Henry Vaughan's poems also take an apocalyptic view of Jonson's presence. After Vaughan graduated from Oxford he spent a short time in London and fought briefly in the Civil Wars before he returned to his native Wales where English was a "foreign" language.[6] He opened his first published collection of poems by casting off "Distracts of the Towne" (l. 3) and looking forward to meeting "Great *B E N*" in the Elysian fields where "learned Ghosts admire" him and long "To catch the subject of his Song" (ll. 30–32). But in *Olor Iscanus* (1651) the timeless rusticity of pastoral poems such as "To the River Isca" is juxtaposed with elegaic ones that express surprise over the sudden fall into history. In "The Charnel House" the dead bodies that provoke the "Eloquent silence" that threatens to overwhelm the poet's tongue turn out to be the books of his "sad library" where he takes notes to record the fragmented details of the political world. Vaughan turned his back on the literary life of London. His poems remain true to the hope that the approaching apocalypse would unite Britons so "That like true sheep, all in one fold/ We may be fed, and one mind hold" (S-134, ll. 47–48). The popular literacy fostered by print subverts the purity of oral prophecy in poems such as "The Wreath" (S-130) where the speaker is both "an exemplary *reader* of God's *book* and an *emblem* of the illuminated soul" (Post 1982, 152–53, my emphasis).

Andrew Marvell's "Horatian Ode" is similarly informed by Jonson's ambivalent attempts to mediate between excess and restraint. And in Marvell's "Tom May's Death," Jonson appears as a spokesman for the loss of the "antient Rights" lamented in the Ode (l. 30). The first thing the poem tells us is that May died drunk. When he arrived in Elysium he saw a fat man whom he imagined to be Ares but who turned out to be Jonson. When Jonson saw May he stopped singing of "ancient Heroes," gently signified that he was wrong to praise May for his translation of Lucan's *Pharsalia*, and proceeded to parody the striking sexual opening lines of that translation in which the warrior woman, great Rome, "distains/ In her owne bowels her victorious swords" (11.2–3), to read that May himself sheaths "In his own Bowels . . . the conquering health" (l. 24).

In other words, May's debauchery renders him incapable of "celebrating"—both sexually and poetically—the feminine muse. By pouring numerous cups of wine "In his own Bowels," his only intercourse is with himself. Instead of being ashamed of this impotence, May attempts to insinuate himself into "the Learned throng" (l. 28), but Jonson, with his phallic "Laurel wand" (l. 33), expels him because he was basely "prostituted . . . /Our spotless knowledge" (ll. 71–72). Thus the debauched May is "only Master of these Revels past" (l. 98). The last lines of the poem, where May vanishes "in a Cloud of pitch,/ Such as unto the Sabboth bears the Witch" (ll. 99–100), echo the eighth charm uttered by the witches in *The Masque of Queenes*, and question May's gender identity. This castrated and marginalized poet, once the star of his time, is what the speaker fears he himself, as a representative intellectual/artist, might become. By moving toward legitimacy—that is, by seeking to have "his work" accepted, by publishing "his work"—the "life" depicted in these texts became representative. In resistance to this representative status—this identification with the status quo and the patriarchal power structure—authors increasingly pictured themselves and their heroes as pathetic figures, forever alienated and nostalgic, searching for an imaginary lost wholeness.

At the beginning of the nineteenth century, Hegel borrowed the concept of the *belle âme* (die schöne seele) or "beautiful soul" from Goethe and used it to explain this phenomenon (1977, pars. 658–68). As Anthony Wilden has noted, this concept is epitomized by Robin Hood, who is identified with the theme of "the individual versus society." But this, Wilden explains, is a dangerous situation for "The heartfelt identification with the universal well being of humanity by the individual governed by the law of the heart passes into madness . . . when he discovers the opposition and indifference to his good intentions of those he wishes to save from themselves" (1968, 297–88). As Wilden further points out,

> Hegel is dealing with a whole tradition of the Romantic "literature of the self," beginning with Rousseau's great novel, the *Confessions*, and including Goethe's *Werther*, . . . and the Karl Moor of Schiller's *Brigands* (whose prototype may be found in Diderot's *contes*). These characters are inevitably linked to the master and the slave, to the noble and the base consciousness (287).

There is little wonder that Nietzsche contemptuously refered to the "Utterly depraved 'spirits,' 'beautiful souls'" who consider his books "*beneath* themselves" (1989, 264).

In rebellion against perceived restraint, which calls for the sublimation of libidinal energies, such a figure strives for release, for spontaneity. At the same time he yearns to recapture a previous state of communal bliss. The beautiful soul is, again in Wilden's words, a schizoid personality: his fundamental question is the question of his being in an expressly existential sense. He not only asks: "What am I in my being?" but he fears the loss of the very void he discovers he is. His relationship to being-in-the-world and to being-with-others can very aptly be characterized as the "splitting of the ego" (the self)—into many possible "parts." . . . The *belle âme* fears the other because he wants so much to be the other, but being the other means losing himself. . . . Thus the *belle âme* refuses necessary alienation and becomes more or less estranged from others and from the world as a result. (290–91).

In Foucault's *Discipline and Punish*, this beautiful soul is seen as part of an aestheticization of criminality:

in appearance, it is the discovery of the beauty and greatness of crime; in fact, it is the affirmation that greatness too has a right to crime and that it even becomes the exclusive privilege of those who are really great. . . . The split was complete; the people was robbed of its own pride in its crimes. (1979, 68–69)[7]

The split between the persona of the author and that of the implied narrator, which reflects the psychological split between individual desire and the Other who holds out the promise of the fulfillment of desire, looks forward to the end of an historico-metaphysical epoch. In this epoch, as Derrida has demonstrated,

Writing in the common sense is the dead letter, it is the carrier of death. It exhausts life. . . . [But] the other face of the same proportion, writing in the metaphoric sense, natural, divine, and living writing, is venerated; it is equal in dignity to the origin of value, to the voice of conscience as divine law. . . . There is therefore a good and a bad writing: the good and natural is the divine inscription in the heart and the soul; the perverse and artful is technique, exiled in the exteriority of the body. (1977, 17)

In *The Birth of Tragedy* the opposition between these two forms of writing is reaffirmed with a vengeance.

There, Dionysus is aligned with good writing, with dithy-rambic music (nature), and Apollo is associated with bad writing, with representation and *mimesis* (the attempt to recuperate the spontaneity of lost originary experience). The split authorial "voice" holds out the possibility of a voice that "is not originally subordinate to the logos and to truth." Nietzsche thus moves toward "the absolute ef-facement of the signifier" and sets the stage for "the final writing of an epoch" (Derrida 1977, 19, 20, 23), a writing alluded to and glimpsed at—but never seen—under the authorial name of Gustave von Aschenbach in Thomas Mann's *Death in Venice.*

In Mann's story, repressed Dionysianism erupts in the psyche of an Apollonian author who attempts to fix living speech in deathless prose, who devotes his life to constructing a monument to unaging intellect. The story recuperates the Robin Hood legend as read through He-gel's beautiful soul topos. Aschenbach sees the 14 year-old Tadzio as an embodiment of perfect form comparable to that which his own writing has attained: "Was not the same force at work in himself when he strove in cold fury to liberate from the marble mass of language the slender forms of his art . . . ?" (Mann 1954, 44) In this Horatian reverie, Aschenbach is transported back to ancient Athens where he recalls a conversation from the *Phaedrus*, after which he has a desire to "write in Tadzio's presence" (46). But after Tadzio smiles a Narcissian smile, Aschenbach finds himself, as Claudius finds Hamlet, "quite unmanned" (52). "Driven by his mania," a passion which "is like crime [because] it does not thrive on the established order and common round; it welcomes every blow dealt the bour-geois structure, every weakening of the social fabric" (54), Aschenbach, "drunk with . . . deamonic power" (55), be-comes a solitary outcast who sacrifices himself and Tad-zio—whom he could have saved from the cholera—and loses himself in a fearful Dionysian dream.

This dream begins with a recapitulation of "a kind of howl, with a long-drawn *u*-sound at the end" (67), the same sound Aschenbach originally associated with Tadzio's name (32). And as the troops of human forms dance and run after goats, Aschenbach hears all of the mad rout yelling "that cry, composed of soft consonants with a long-drawn *u*-sound at the end, so sweet and wild it was together, and like nothing ever heard before!" (67). As an archetypal negation, this statement succeeds in affirming that which it denies, succeeds in drawing our attention to the fact that Aschenbach heard this sound when he first heard Tadzio's name.

Of course we recall the scene where Aschenbach first heard Tadzio's name, but this also suggests a prior remembrance for Aschenbach *as well as for us*, a remembrance similar to that evoked—but not articulated—by the "long-drawn-out 'o-o-o-o', accompanied by an expression of interest and satisfaction" that Freud's grandson made when he was observed to play the *fort/da* game (*Freud 1955a, 14*). The sound Aschenbach hears enables us to recall *for him* the primal sound of longing, the "gone" or "adieu" that the sound of Tadzio's name first suggests to Aschenbach and that is later ("later" in the text and in remembrance but primal and therefore *prior* in ontogeny) "heard" in the dream in which Aschenbach's repressed Dionysianism returns to his psyche.[8] In this primal myth of high modernism, the marginalization of women in general—and of the mother in particular—is a metonomy for the discovery and creation of self in popular culture.

Such beautiful souls are everywhere apparent in the canonical texts of high modernism. This figure evolved through Wertherism, Byronism, Rimbaudism, and may be found in the work of Gide, Proust, Mann, Joyce—whose persona, Stephen Dedalus, adopts Ben Jonson as a hero —and especially in the autobiographical works of Jean Genet. This beautiful soul is paradigmatic of the romantic, rebellious intellectual/artist in popular culture. Variously depicted in novels, films, television series, and in the personae of innumerable "pop" music stars as the "good" outlaw, some of the beautiful soul's epigones would include Hollywood versions of Jesse James and the public personae created both on and offscreen for James Dean, Marlon Brando, and Mickey Rourke.

All of the major Hollywood films ostensibly based on the legends of Maid Marian and Robin Hood firmly defend patriarchal values and maintain stereotypical gender roles. In Douglas Fairbanks's swashbuckling silent *Robin Hood* (1922), the most expensive and most popular film of its time, Maid Marian has no real part at all; in *The Adventures of Robin Hood* (1938), with a dashing Errol Flynn, Olivia deHaviland is a demure damsel in distress; in the lacrymose *Robin and Marian* (1976) Sean Connery and Audrey Hepburn are a nostalgic middle–aged couple; and in *Robin Hood: Prince of Thieves* (1991), which features a dour Kevin Costner as Robin of Locksley Hall, Mary Elizabeth Mastrantonio is a plucky but very proper Maid Marian.[9] In *Thelma and Louise* (1991), Susan Sarandon and Geena Davies subvert patriarchal values and undermine gender stereotypes in a spirit much closer to that of the legendary Marian and Robin.

Hollywood has occasionally captured something like the carnivalesque spirit of the legendary Marian and Robin in films about outlaw heterosexual couples. In *Bonnie and Clyde* (1967), Faye Dunnaway and Warren Beatty challenge stereotypical gender roles in the same way Jonson's Marian and Robin do; in *Badlands* (1973), Sissy Spacek relates to Martin Sheen's melancholy misfit in a similar manner; and in Steven Spielberg's *Sugarland Express* (1974), a vitally subversive Goldie Hawn is contrasted to a passive Ben Johnson. But the alienation that results from the encounter between the artistic temperament and the perceived realities of the middle class is more radically deconstructed in Manuel Puig's *Kiss of the Spider Woman* (1980), which was made into a film directed by Hector Babencoa starring William Hurt, Raul Julia, and Sylvia Braga in 1985. Here the Robin Hood figure—the outlaw/homosexual in rebellion against the feminine within himself and against the repressed femininity in middle-class society—is split into two characters who exhibit Otherness. The disciplined and sexually repressed intellectual, Valentin, is a dedicated revolutionary, an urban guerrilla, who wants to overthrow the colonels. He finds himself in an Argentine prison with the imaginative and pleasure-seeking artist, Molina, who passes his time in prison by escaping into the illusory world of movies, and who, when Valentin accuses him of being "a regular bourgeois gentle-man at heart" corrects him by saying: "Bourgeois lady, thank you" (Puig 1980, 44).

Despite Molina's desire for conventional respectability, his homosexuality and his hedonism alienate him from the norms of middle-class society more radically than Valentin's radical politics do him. Molina compromises his mind, his intellect, by accepting the pleasures of escapism that popular culture offers; Valentin rejects such diversions, but in so doing he compromises his body, his sensuality. Molina has not completely separated himself from his childlike attachment to his mother, and his feelings toward her are passionately protective as well as boldly sentimental. Valentin, on the other hand, has tried, without success, to liberate himself from monogamy and from Marta, the upper-middle-class woman he loves and whose identity is merged with his own when Valentin recognizes the femininity he has repressed in himself in his post-torture delirium. In the end, after Valentin and Molina make love, their positions reverse. Molina is released and is killed as he tries to deliver a message from Valentin to his friends in the underground revolutionary movement. Valentin "escapes" into a drug-induced world of fantasy where he sails away with his haute bourgeois dream woman.

The double hero—Chamcha/Gibreel—of Salman Rushdie's *Satanic Verses* (1989) is another such parodic representative of the beautiful soul and of the entire Western conception of the author, of authorization, and of the very idea of *sacred* texts. Such deconstructions of the myth of wholeness make it possible to see that the split subjectivity of the beautiful soul can never be healed. But this is not a nihilistic conclusion. The author-function is ana-chronistic in a postmodern culture of simulation. Where there is no God, no *presence*, no transcendent "voice"—and no fixed essential selfhood—for an author to simulate, there is no transcendental or absolute truth to represent, no authenticity behind the sign. No longer can a master artist allow the rebellious woman to spin her web of puckish delusion, to create images, representations that veil the phallus. That delusion was fed by a utopian belief in the attainment of complete autonomy, the *causa sui* project by which humans deny their connectedness to the Other and act as though they are self-created beings. There is no better answer to such pathetic arrogance than De-meter's laughter at Baubo's obscene gesture. As Bakhtin observes at the end of his great book:

> The exceptional freedom and pitiless gaiety of the Rabelai-sian image were possible only on the confines of languages.
> Thus we see that in Rabelais freedom of laughter, con-secrated by the tradition of popular-festive forms, was raised to a higher level of ideological consciousness, thanks to the victory over linguistic dogmatism. (1984, 473)

Notes

Notes to Introduction

1. Also relevant here is Renate Lachmann's discussion of how Bakhtin saw "in the Renaissance not only the fusion of a carnivalized antiquity and the folk culture of the Middle Ages but also a historically 'unique' amalgamation of high culture and folk culture" (1989, 139), and Dominick LaCapra's discussion of the "hermetic appropriation of the carnivalesque" (1989, 25ff).

2. My use of the concept of appropriation is indebted to Robert Weimann's discussion in " 'Appropriation' and Modern History" and "Text, Author-Function, and Appropriation" and to essays by Douglas Crimp and Meaghan Morris.

3. See especially the essays "Intellectuals in Education," and "Observations on Folklore," and the section on "Popular Culture" in *An Antonio Gramsci Reader* (1988, 300–22, 350–53, 360–78).

4. I find much to applaud in Lawrence Venuti's critique of old and new historicist readings of Renaissance texts, but I do not think it possible, nor even desirable, to develop a methodology that would "bring back the past as the past" (Venuti 1989, 263).

5. David Quint has provided a cogent summary of how poststructuralism has problematized the concept of authorship at the start of the modern era. He explains how the author-function was based on the premise that reading was a "process of self-creation" by which and through which a person was led "to discover and create his [sic] own identity," a unique, fixed, intrinsic individuality (1986, 3).

6. Foucault notes that "Texts, books, and discourses really began to have authors (other than mythical, 'sacralized' and 'sacralizing' figures) to the extent that authors became subject to punishment, that is, to the extent that discourses could be transgressive" (1984, 108).

David Riggs concludes his recent biography of Jonson by disagreeing with Foucault's statement that the author-function is "the principle of thrift in the proliferation of meaning" (Foucault

1984, 118–19). "On the contrary," Riggs states, "the institution of authorship created a context in which Jonson's transgressive texts could circulate freely despite official opposition to his work. The role of author helped to enfranchise displaced intellectuals" (Riggs 1989, 353). Riggs fails to see that Foucault is talking about *authorship*, not *print*.

Implications of Foucault's essay are discussed in essays by Nancy K. Miller, Jacqueline Rose, and Margaret W. Ferguson in the anthology edited by Elizabeth Weed. And Cheryl Walker has boldly and perceptively confronted the question asked in Foucault's title.

Following Foucault, Timothy Reiss has demonstrated how the new practice of writing and knowledge exercised a disciplinary function over culture in the seventeenth century. Richard Helgerson, Margaret W. Ferguson, and Jonathan Crewe have explored the images of transgression around humanist notions of authorship, and David Saunders and Ian Hunter have argued that "intense inwardness" should be attributed to the role of literacy "in an ethical practice through whose mastery writers could compose themselves as subjects" (1991, 509).

Notes to Chapter One

1. Theodore A. Stroud has suggested that the priest who converted Jonson was Thomas Wright, author of *The Passions of the Minde in Generall* (1604), for which Jonson wrote a dedicatory sonnet. I have discussed the significance of Jonson's conversion to Catholicism in greater detail in my essay on "Ben Jonson's Libertine Catholicism."

2. Jonson's admirer John Taylor the Water Poet noted many alliances between Catholicism, witchcraft, and other forms of political and doctrinal subversion in his works. For other examples of the link between Catholicism and subversion, see Davies 1947, 20ff; Walker 1981, 44–46; and Ingram 1985, 129–31.

3. Gramsci noted how materialism, "common sense," "popular superstition," and witchcraft could all "be seen in popular Catholicism" (1988, 352). Florence M. Weinberg emphasizes this aspect of Catholicism in her study of Rabelais, as does J. Delumean in his discussion of "folklorized Christianity."

4. As early as 1666, Margaret of Newcastle explained how Jonson based Subtle on Dee, Face on Kelley, and Dol on their wives (H&S 11.47).

5. There is also here an implied parody of the Elizabethan cult of chivalry (as well as the Catholic cult of the virgin) in the

reference to Spenser's portrait of the pure Una, who is contrasted with the Catholic whore Duessa.

6. C. E. Bennett provides the following translation: "I have finished a monument more lasting than bronze and loftier than the pyramids' royal pile, one that no wasting rain, no furious north wind can destroy, or the countless chain of years and the ages' flight. I shall not altogether die, but a mighty part of me shall escape the death-goddess. On and on shall I grow, ever fresh with the glory of after time." As Norman O. Brown has pointed out, the Ode expresses "the hope of the man who has not lived, whose life has been spent conquering death, whose life has passed into those immortal pages" (1959, 287). Walter J. Ong has seen the Ode as the *locus classicus* of death in the text (1977, 237–38), and Michael C. J. Putnam has written that "History's progress . . . has no effect, in Horace's view, on the mind's autocratic, apocalyptic creations" (1982, 137).

7. Shakespeare's Sonnet 55:

Not marble, nor the guilded monuments
Of princes, shall outlive this powerful rhyme,

is also often cited as an analogue of Horace's image of his poetry as a monument. Thus T. S. Eliot wrote about "The existing monuments" of tradition that "form an ideal order among themselves" in "Tradition and the Individual Talent" (1920b, 50).

8. H&S add another poem, a translation from Martial celebrating sobriety and chastity, which Jonson did not include in the collection.

9. The classical statement of this analogy is Seneca's Epistle 84, which is quoted and discussed by Robert M. Durling in his essay "Deceit and Digestion in the Belly of Hell" (1981, 62). As Richard S. Peterson has observed, the analogy is more than a strange anomaly, for to Jonson "bad imitation is personified as a 'Creature' that in its indiscriminate eagerness to eat literally swallows everything whole, without any equipment to digest it; whereas good imitation has not only a healthy 'Appetite,' . . . but a sophisticated means of dealing with what it consumes" (1981, 8). Don K. Hedrick catalogued many examples of cannibalism "and its adjunctive Bacchic frenzy" (1977, 233) in Jonson's plays. In Dekker's *Satiromastix* (1601), where Jonson appears as Horace, he is asked: "Art not famous enough yet . . . for killing a player, but thou must eate men alive?" (1964, 4.2.61–62).

10. Peterson cites this passage as evidence that the term "reconciled" could mean "a subordination, a submission to a higher authority such as the church (OED)" (1981, 131).

11. Jonson told Drummond that Elizabeth's hymen was so

tough it was impossible for any man to have intercourse with her, "though for her delight she tryed many," and that "there was a French Chirurgion who took in hand to cut it, yet fear stayed her & his death" (*Conv*. 342–46).

12. Jacques Lacan explains his use of the phrase "name-of-the-father" in "The Function of Language" (1968, 41 and 126n96); see also, in the same volume, Anthony Wilden's essay "Lacan and the Discourse of the Other" (270ff).

13. Elizabeth Eisenstein has explained how George Sarton "undermined his positive thesis" that print "replaced precarious forms of tradition (oral and manuscript) by one that was stable, secure and lasting" (1978, 507–08ff). And Natalie Zemon Davis has pointed out that "Economic control of publishing was not concentrated in the houses of great merchant-publishers, but was shared by a variety of producers. Monopolies in knowledge had broken down but had not [yet] been replaced by effective political and religious censorship and by the theory and laws of private property in ideas" (1975, 225–26). James A. Boon succinctly articulates one effect of popular literacy when he observes that "Advocates of direct understanding of Scripture rejected 'divine right' for both appointed bishops and hereditary kings" (1982, 169).

Notes to Chapter Two

1. Jo Ann Hoeppner Moran has documented the effects of the expansion of elementary and grammar education on the priesthood in the fourteenth, fifteenth, and early sixteenth centuries.

2. Robert Muchembled has argued that witchcraft persecutions were an effort to repress an element of folk culture that would not submit to the new absolutist state. I owe this reference to Tara McGann who has developed Muchembled's argument with reference to Althusser and Lacan.

3. As Jonas Barish has remarked, Nietzsche himself "lovingly and nostalgically evoked" Attic theater in *The Birth of Tragedy* as "a moment of unrecoverable splendor" (1981, 417).

4. Cf. Thomas M. Greene's "Ben Jonson and the Centered Self," and the counterarguments by Richard S. Peterson (1981, 25–29) and William E. Cain in "Self and Others in Two Poems by Ben Jonson."

5. John Marston's 1599 revision of this comedy, which includes a satiric portrait of Jonson, should not be confused with the Puritan William Prynne's 1633 attack on the theater under the same title.

6. Both plays were entered in the Stationers' Register on 1 December 1600. Philip Henslowe, Jonson's employer, paid Munday for them in February and March 1598 (D&T 220–21), and they were acted by the Admiral's Company that year (Gilman 1972, 843). An earlier play, *The Pastoral Comedy, or Robin Hood and Little John*, entered in the Register on 14 May 1594, is now lost, but it may have been the same as the anonymous *Robin Hood and Little John* that was extant in 1624 and 1640 (D&T 22n2).

7. The play was based on a prose romance, *The Famous History of George a Greene*, and on the famous ballad *The Jolly Pinder of Wakefield*. An earlier ballad on this same figure was entered in the Stationers' Register in 1557–58. Dobson and Taylor suggest that, like Maid Marian, George a Greene probably became attached to the Robin Hood legend "through the agency of the May Games" (1976, 147).

8. The quotations in this paragraph are from the anonymous contemporary account entitled, in part, *The Wonderfull Discoverie of the Witch-crafts of Margaret and Philip Flower, Daughters of Joan Flower Neere Bever Castle: Executed at Lincolne. . . .* London, 1619. Eller provides further details and quotes extensively from the contemporary account (1841, 61–66).

9. Laura Levine has shown how the attacks on theatricality "grow increasingly obsessed with the idea of the effeminized man—the thing that has no inherent nature because it has no inherent gender and is monstrous precisely because of this fact" (1986, 130); see also Jean-Christophe Agnew's discussion of Puritan reactions to theatrical crossdressing (1986, 128–35), and Jean E. Howard's review of research on this topic.

10. De Worde printed the earliest known edition of *The Lyttell Gest of Robin Hode* c. 1510, to which Jonson had access in the collection of his friend John Selden.

11. Eric Havelock has explained how this passage relates to Plato's concept of *mimesis* (1963, ch. 2), and Jacques Derrida has problematized the conventional analysis of *mimesis* in "The Double Session" (1972, see esp. 186n14).

12. Fineman explains that "it would be possible to trace out in recent theoretical discussion, especially discussion of subjectivity, a development very similar not only to the development that we can discern in Shakespeare's sonnets . . . but similar also to the larger literary development within which we can locate the historical significance of Shakespeare's sonnet sequence as a whole. For example, responding to Husserl's Dantesque phenomenology of *Ideas*, to Husserl's concern with eidetic reduction and a transcendental Ego, Sartre developed a psychology of imagination whose logic and figurality very much resemble the

paranoic visionary thematics of at least some of Shakespeare's
... sonnets" (1985, 45).

Notes to Chapter Three

1. Annabel Patterson has critiqued the monologic readings
of pastoral by Stephen Orgel and Anthony Low and Williams's
reading of "To Penshurst." As she notes: "There is a whole range
of eccentric responses *within* the hegemonic corpus, intima-
tions of doubt, criticisms of self or of the monarch or of the
socio-political system. . . . It is well to bear in mind, therefore,
the potentially liberating alternative model defined by Bakhtin"
(1987, 139–49). My approach differs from Patterson's in that I do
not privilege authorial intention and "original" context as ways
of fixing a text's meaning; on this point see Saunders and Hunter
(1991, 486–87).

2. Susan Stewart's misquotation of the third word of the poem,
changing it from "not" to "now" (1984, 63), indicates how powerful the tendency is to make, to force, the poem into the categories of ordinary discourse, to make the poem say what we sup-
pose or assume such a poem *should* say.

3. René Girard has theorized about the significance of these
practices as they are represented in Euripides's *Bacchae* (1977,
130–32), Marcel Detienne provides further information in regard to omophagy as a kind of communal feast (1979, 62–63, 88),
and Carlo Ginzburg has examined such practices in relation to
witchcraft and the Sabbat (1991, 226–97).

4. Bakhtin cites Adam de la Halle's *Play in the Bower*, "the
first medieval comic play that has been preserved," as "a remark-
able example of a purely carnivalesque vision and conception of
the world" (1984, 15).

5. Cressy says "the over-all illiteracy of husbandmen in pre-
industrial England was close to 80%" (1980, 156). Nottingham-
shire—the setting of *The Sad Shepherd*—had the highest illiteracy in all of England, with three-fourths of the adult males
being unable to sign their names in the period 1638–44 (74–75).

6. Despite the fact that he was found guilty of treason for
casting aspersions on Queene Anne and was imprisoned and
had his ears cut off, in 1636 Prynne followed up his attack on
the stage with *Divine Tragedie lately acted, or a Collection of
sundry memorable examples of Gods Judgements upon Sab-
bath-breakers.*

7. Richard A. Burt has noted that "The status of the puppet
show is . . . clearly equivocal, open equally to the antithetical

views that it is licensed and that it is licentious. Like the Fair, the puppet show licenses the subversion of the distinctions—of gender, class, and aesthetics—on which the social order is based, and with its license produces social disorder" (1987, 534).

8. On Dover, see Marcus 1986, 132, 155.

Notes to Chapter Four

1. Freud discusses this process in "Further Remarks on the Neuro-Psychoses of Defence" (1955c, 166–67n2); and in "From the History of an Infantile Neurosis" (1955b, 45n1). Dominick LaCapra has explored this concept in relation to the development of "a new [Lacanian] rhetoric (whose end is not yet in sight)" (1989, 34–35).

2. It is quite possible that Jonson had read *Sir Gawain and the Green Knight* by the time he wrote *The Sad Shepherd*. The unique manuscript in which it is found passed from Henry Savile (1568–1617), to whom Jonson addressed *Ep.* XCV, to Robert Cotton, whose library Jonson used extensively.

3. The Oxford editors note that Jonson's use of this dialect is "inconsistent" and "amateurish" because it includes "spurious and impossible forms" (H&S 10.363). But of course this serves to call attention to it as "unnatural."

4. Peggy Knapp has explored this theme in relation to Jonson's efforts "To castigate the 'publicke riot' caused by capitalism" (1979, 580) in his major plays.

5. In ancient Greece, Dionysian worship was predominantly feminine (Farnell 1896–1909, 5.159–61), and, according to J. P. Vernant, essentially "une experience religieuse inverse du culte officiel" (1965, 268).

6. John Guillory has pointed out that "In Renaissance medical texts, the garrulity of women is said to be the result of hysteria (in the root sense)" (1986, 343n23). Stallybrass analyzes the connection between speaking and wantonness in his essay on "Patriarchal Territories" (1986, 126–29). The significance of hysteria is discussed more fully in chapter five.

7. D. P. Walker has noted that Galen said that hysteria in men was "caused by retention of semen due to excessive sexual abstinence" (1981, 13). Freud often said he himself was a hysteric.

8. Margot Heinemann has discussed Middleton's borrowings from Jonson (1980, 106–07).

9. Jonson mentions Forman in *Epicoene* (4.1.150) and in *The Devil Is An Ass* (2.8.33), where the Overbury murder is alluded to in some detail.

10. The scandal has been much written about. Beatrice White has published the most comprehensive account. David Lindley has recently cited reports that the examination to test Lady Frances's virginity "was fixed by substituting another girl in her place," and he says that "There is some evidence that Frances was indeed the virgin she claimed to be," but he does not say what that evidence is (1986, 346 and n6). Margaret Heinemann says that the opposition to the Howard/Carr marriage was led by "Puritans" (1980, 107–08), and David Norbrook notes that "The misogyny that often lay behind Puritan insistence on strict female virtue could be felt in the many denunciations of Frances Howard's wantonness" (1984, 207).

Notes to Chapter Five

1. Waldron is even more explicit; he adds *"Enter Maudlin, the witch, as Marian."*
2. The hare, as Marcel Detienne has shown, "plays a complex role in his relations with the divinities of sexuality. His amorous temperament qualifies him as an effective gift between male lovers for whom intrigue cannot be divorced from hunting. In addition, his timidity and fearful nature predispose his serving as an emblem for the shy object of lust. Finally, his prolific nature assures him of a privileged place in the domain of fertility ruled within marriage, at least in part, by the Aphrodite of Persuasion and the bond of love" (1979, 49).
3. According to Tuberville, the short erect tail of a hare is called a scut.
4. Robert Weimann has traced the history of Robin Goodfellow as a folk hero (1978, 192–96), and Maurice Keen has discussed the mythological theory, often associated with the work of Margaret Murray, that conflates the legend of Robin Hood with that of Robin Goodfellow. Keen points out "serious problems" with this argument, but he concludes that "it is just possible" (1961, 219–22); see also Ginzburg's discussion (1991, 3–9).
5. Foucault's theory of discourse is summarized in the opening chapters of *The Archeology of Knowledge.* Pecheux's theorization is at evidence in *Language, Semantics and Ideology.*
6. "The mother" was the commonly used term for hysteria. Lear laments: "O, how this mother swells up toward my heart!/ Hysterica passio, down, thou climbing sorrow,/ Thy element's below" (2.4.92). And in "An Epigram on The Court Purcell," Jonson wrote that "They say you weekly invite fits o'th'Mother,/ And practice for a Miracle" (ll. 40–41).

7. Luce Irigaray has examined the concept of hysteria in Western metaphysics under the title "Plato's *Hysteria*" (1985, 243–364). According to Jean Baudrillard, "Hysteria was the pathology of the exacerbated staging of the subject, a pathology of expression of the body's theatrical and operatic conversion" (1983, 132).

8. Raymond Urban has argued that "Since Jonson wrote three masques in Frances's honor and had her play in two others, we must expect him to take her part, portraying her not as the nasty young lady that she was but as an unlucky beauty shackled to a clumsy, rustic lord." Urban believes Lady Frances was the model for Earine and Essex was the model for Lorel. According to him, Jonson made Earine and Douce "look-alikes" because he thought ordinary people could not "pierce the veil of rumor and illusion" and see the difference "between a young witch and a captive, persecuted maiden." As Urban would have it, "the irony, of course, is that the vulgar beliefs were correct. The undiscerning ones were the great witch-experts, Ben Jonson and King James, who did not recognize the real witch hidden behind her veil of court prestige" (1975, 308–09). Thus Urban condemns Jonson for holding a foolish opinion that Urban attributes to him based on his own monovocal interpretation of Jonson's intentions.

9. Macduff, like Athena, is "none of woman born" (*Macbeth* 4.1.80); cf. Dianne Hunter's reading of *Macbeth*, in relationship to the *Bacchae*, as a patriarchal myth in "Doubling, Mythic Difference, and the Scapegoating of Female Power in *Macbeth*" and Marjorie Garber's analysis of *Macbeth* as a male Medusa.

In the folk play *Robin Hood and the Knight*, based on the ballad "Robin Hood and Guy of Gisborne," Robin Hood kills the knight, cuts off his head, and disguises himself in the knight's clothes.

10. Here "Copy" means pattern or example, what Baudrillard calls a first order of simulation (1983, 83ff); cf. Shakespeare's *King John* (4.2.113) and *All's Well* (1.2.46).

11. Cf. Freud's footnote on the fear of castration in *Totem and Taboo* (1955g, 152) and the discussion of the terror of the head of the Medusa as an apotropaic symbol of the female genitalia and thus, to men, of the fear of castration, in his essay on "Medusa's Head" (1955e, 273–74).

12. Cf. Habermas's charge that "to instrumental reason [poststructuralists] juxtapose in Manichean fashion a principle only accesible through evocation, be it the will to power or sovereignty, Being or the Dionysiac force of the poetical" (1983, 14).

Notes to Epilogue

1. See especially Clément's explanation, via Levi-Strauss and Michelet, of how the Freudian myth of origin is inverted by the Sabbat as a festival of "endogamous love" (1986, 30–31).

2. I have in mind here not only the disruption of acceptance of masculine pronouns as generic but also the undermining of so-called Standard English as the only acceptable model of usage in popular culture.

3. Lawrence Stone has observed that during the last half of the sixteenth century the relative authority of the husband over his wife was growing. "A woman's legal right to hold and dispose of her own property was limited to what she could specifically lay claim to in a marriage contract. By marriage, the husband and wife became one person in law—and that person was the husband. He acquired absolute control of all his wife's personal property, which he could sell at will. . . . A husband always had full rights . . . over his wife's real estate" (1979, 136).

4. It should be noted that McLuskie castigates Jonson for "His sarcastic outrage at women's pretensions to learning or religious enthusiasm" and "his passionate contempt for their attempts to regulate their sexuality or to find a direct access to creativity" as well as "the more fundamental misogyny which lay at the heart of his satiric vision" (1989, 191).

David Underdown has noted that "The witch and the scold had risen together as alienated outsiders, casualties of a changing social order; when a different kind of order was consolidated its defenders found less need to discipline them" (1985, 286–87). And as Clément has explained, the reason there was "less need" is because the hysteric, unlike the witch, "is a prisoner inside the family" (1986, 8).

5. Zera S. Fink has shown how this ideal informs seventeenth century texts.

6. M. M. Mahood has noted that Vaughans's "compatriot, Miss Gwenllian Morgan, was convinced that the Silurist habitually thought in Welsh; and the feeling of beginning a new language, which we experience in reading Vaughan, may in part be due to the fact that English was not his mother-tongue" (1970, 253).

7. As David Carroll explains after he quotes this passage: "The difference, then, is between two 'aesthetics': the first a disruptive, popular aesthetics whose 'beauty' is in the cruelty of the acts being recounted; the second is an aesthetics of the 'fine arts,' which makes the criminal a 'great man,' a 'genius,' thus elevating him above the public sphere and eliminating

the threat he poses to it by keeping him at a safe distance from it" (1987, 124).

8. Lee Quinby and I have explored this aspect of Mann's story in "The Aporia of the Bourgeois Artist" (1989).

9. Four films were produced for British television under the general heading *Robin Hood: The Legend* in the mid-1980s. *Robin Hood and the Sorcerer*, directed by Ian Sharp, and *The Swords of Wayland*, directed by Robert M. Young, appeared in 1983, and *Herne's Son*, directed by Robert M. Young, and *The Time of the Wolfe*, directed by Syd Roberson, appeared in 1985.

Works Cited

Agnew, Jean-Christophe. (1986). *Worlds Apart: The Market and the Theater in Anglo-American Thought, 1550–1750*. Cambridge: Cambridge University Press.

Bakhtin, Mikhail. (1968). *Rabelais and His World*. (Helene Iswolsky, trans.). Bloomington: Indiana University Press; repr. 1984.

Bal, Mieke. (1987). *Lethal Love: Feminist Literary Readings of Biblical Love Stories*. Bloomington: University of Indiana Press.

Barber, C. L. (1959). *Shakespeare's Festive Comedy: A Study of Dramatic Form and Its Relation to Social Custom*. Cleveland: Meridian; repr. 1963.

Barish, Jonas A. (1981). *The Antitheatrical Prejudice*. Berkeley: University of California Press.

———. (1960). *Ben Jonson and the Language of Prose Comedy*. New York: Norton; repr. 1970.

Barton, Anne. (1984). *Ben Jonson, Dramatist*. Cambridge: Cambridge University Press.

Baudrillard, Jean. (1983a). "The Ecstasy of Communication." (John Johnston, trans.). In *The Anti-Aesthetic: Essays on Postmodern Culture*. (Hal Foster, ed.). Port Townsend, WA: Bay Press, 126–34.

———. (1983b). "The Orders of Simulacra." (Philip Beitchman, trans.). In *Simulations*. New York: Semiotext(e), 83–159.

Baxter, P. T. W. (1972). "Absence Makes the Heart Grow Fonder: Some Suggestions why Witchcraft Accusations are Rare among East African Pastoralists." In *The Allocation of Responsibility*. (M. Gluckman, ed.). Manchester: Manchester University Press.

Bellamy, John. (1985). *Robin Hood: An Historical Inquiry*. Bloomington: Indiana University Press.

Bennett, C. E., trans. and ed. (1934). *Horace: Odes and Epodes*. (John C. Rolfe, rev.). Boston: Loeb Classical Library, Harvard University Press.

Bennett, Tony. (1979). *Formalism and Marxism.* New York: Methuen.

———. (1986a). "Hegemony, Ideology, Pleasure: Blackpool." In *Popular Culture and Social Relations.* (Tony Bennett, Colin Mercer, and Janet Woollacott, eds.). Philadelphia: Open University Press, 135–54.

———. (1986b). "Introduction: Popular Culture and 'the turn to Gramsci.' " In *Popular Culture and Social Relations.* (Tony Bennett, Colin Mercer, and Janet Woollacott, eds.). Philadelphia: Open University Press, xi–xix.

Berman, Morris. (1981). *The Reenchantment of the World.* New York: Bantam Books; repr. 1984.

Boehrer, Bruce Thomas. (1990). "Renaissiance Overeating: The Sad Case of Ben Jonson." *PMLA* 105:1069–82.

Boon, James A. (1982). *Other Tribes, Other Scribes: Symbolic Anthropology in the Comparative Study of Cultures, Histories, Religions, and Texts.* Cambridge: Cambridge University Press.

Bordo, Susan. (1987). *The Flight to Objectivity: Essays on Cartesianism and Culture.* Albany: State University of New York Press.

Briggs, Julia. (1983). *This Stage-Play World: English Literature and Its Background, 1580–1625.* Oxford: Oxford University Press.

Bristol, Michael D. (1985). *Carnival and Theater: Plebian Culture and the Structure of Authority in Renaissance England.* New York: Methuen.

Broadbent, John, ed. (1974). *Signet Classic Poets of the 17th Century.* Vol. 2. New York: New American Library.

Brown, Norman O. (1959). *Life Against Death: The Psychoanalytical Meaning of History.* New York: Vintage Books; repr. nd.

Burke, Peter. (1978). *Popular Culture in Early Modern Europe.* New York: New York University Press.

Burt, Richard A. (1987). " 'Licensed by Authority': Ben Jonson and the Politics of Early Stuart Theater." *ELH* 54:529–60.

Butler, Martin. (1984). *Theatre and Crisis, 1632–1642.* Cambridge: Cambridge University Press.

Cain, William E. (1983). "Self and Others in Two Poems by Ben Jonson." *SP* 80:163–82.

Carroll, David. (1987). *Paraesthetics: Foucault, Lyotard, Derrida.* New York: Methuen.

Cixous, Hélène. (1986). "Sorties." In *The Newly Born Woman.* (Betsy Wing, trans.). Minneapolis: University of Minnesota Press, 32–63.

Clark, Stuart. (1977). "King James's *Daemonologie:* Witchcraft and Kingship." In The *Damned Art: Essays in the Literature of Witchcraft.* (Sydney Anglo, ed.). London: Routledge & Kegan Paul, 156–81.

Clément, Catherine. (1986). "The Guilty One." In *The Newly Born Woman.* (Betsy Wing, trans.). Minneapolis: University of Minnesota Press, 3–57.

Clover, Carol J. (1987). "Her Body, Herself: Gender in the Slasher Film." *Representations* 20:187–228.

Coss, P. R. (1985). "Aspects of Cultural Diffusion in Medieval England: The Early Romances, Local Society and Robin Hood." *Past & Present* 108:35–79.

Cox, Gerard H. (1983). "Apocalyptic Projection and the Comic Plot of *The Alchemist.*" *ELR* 13:70–87.

Cressy, David. (1980). *Literacy and the Social Order: Reading and Writing in Tudor and Stuart England.* Cambridge: Cambridge University Press.

Crewe, Jonathan. (1982). *Unredeemed Rhetoric: Thomas Nashe and the Scandal of Authorship.* Baltimore: Johns Hopkins University Press.

Crimp, Douglas. (1982). "Appropriating Appropriation." In *Image Scavengers: Photographs.* Philadelphia: Institute of Contemporary Art, 27–34.

Curtius, Ernst R. (1953). *European Literature and the Latin Middle Ages.* (Willard R. Trask, trans.). New York: Harper & Row; repr. 1963.

Davies, R. Trevor. (1947). *Four Centuries of Witch-Beliefs: With Special Reference to the Great Rebellion.* New York: Benjamin Blom; repr. 1972.

Davis, Natalie Zemon. (1975). *Society and Culture in Early Modern France.* Stanford: Stanford University Press.

de Certeau, Michel. (1986). *Heterologies: Discourse on the Other.* (Brian Massumi, trans.). Minneapolis: University of Minnesota Press.

Dekker, Thomas. (1964). *The Dramatic Works* (Fredson Bowers, ed.). Vol. 1 Cambridge: Cambridge University Press.

de la Halle, Adam. (1872). *Jeu de Robin et de Marion.* In *Oeuvres completes de trouvere Adam de la Halle, poesies et musique.* (E. de Coussemacker, ed.). Farnborough, England: Gregg; repr. 1966. 345–412.

———. (1968). *Le Jeu de la feuillee [par] Adam le Bossu, trouvere artesien de XIIIe siecle.* (Ernest Langlois, ed.). 2nd edn. Paris: Librairie H. Champion.

Delumean, J. (1977). *Catholicism Between Luther and Voltaire.* London.

de Man, Paul. (1979). *Allegories of Reading: Figural Language in*

Rousseau, Nietzsche, Rilke, and Proust. New Haven: Yale University Press.

Derrida, Jacques. (1981). "The Double Session." In *Dissemination.* (Barbara Johnson, trans.). Chicago: University of Chicago Press, 173–286.

———. *Of Grammatology.* (Gayatri Chakravorty Spivak, trans.). Baltimore: Johns Hopkins University Press.

Detienne, Marcel. (1979). *Dionysos Slain.* (Mirielle and Leonard Muellner, trans.). Baltimore: Johns Hopkins University Press.

Dobbs, Betty Jo Teeter. (1975). *The Foundations of Newton's Alchemy.* London: Routledge & Kegan Paul.

Dobson, R. B. and J. Taylor. eds. (1976). *Rymes of Robyn Hood: An Introduction to the English Outlaw.* Pittsburgh: University of Pittsburgh Press.

Donaldson, Ian. (1970). *The World Upside-Down: Comedy from Jonson to Fielding.* Oxford: Clarendon Press.

Drayton, Michael. (1961). *Poly-Olbion.* (J. William Hebel, ed.). Oxford: Shakespeare Head Press, Basil Blackwell.

Durling, Robert M. (1981). "Deceit and Digestion in the Belly of Hell." In *Allegory and Representation.* (Stephen J. Greenblatt, ed.). Baltimore: Johns Hopkins University Press, 61–93.

Eagleton, Terry. (1983). *Literary Theory: An Introduction.* Minneapolis: University of Minnesota Press.

Easthope, Antony. (1982). "Poetry and the Politics of Reading." In *Re-Reading English.* (Peter Widdowson, ed.). New York: Methuen, 136–49.

———. (1983). *Poetry as Discourse.* New York: Methuen.

Eisenstein, Elizabeth L. (1978). *The Printing Press as an Agent of Change: Communications and Cultural Transformations in Early Modern Europe.* Cambridge: Cambridge University Press.

Eliot, T. S. (1920a). "Ben Jonson." In *The Sacred Wood: Essays on Poetry and Criticism.* New York: Methuen, repr. 1986. 104–22.

———. (1920b). "Tradition and the Individual Talent." *In The Sacred Wood: Essays on Poetry and Criticism.* New York: Methuen; repr. 1986. 47–59.

Eller, Irvin. (1841). *The History of Belvoir Castle.* London.

Empson, William. (1935). *Some Versions of Pastoral.* New York: New Directions; repr. 1960.

Farnell, L. R. (1896–1909). *The Cults of the Greek States.* Oxford: Oxford University Press.

Febvre, Lucien, and Henri-Jean Martin. (1976). *The Coming of the Book: The Impact of Printing, 1450–1800.* (David Gerard, trans.). London: New Left Books.

Ferguson, Margaret W. (1981). "Nashe's *The Unfortunate Traveller*: The 'Newes of the Maker' Game," *ELR* 11:165–82.

Fineman, Joel. (1981). "The Structure of Allegorical Desire." In *Allegory and Representation.* (Stephen J. Greenblatt, ed.). Baltimore: Johns Hopkins University Press, 26–60.

———. (1985). *Shakespeare's Perjured Eye: The Invention of Poetic Subjectivity in the Sonnets.* Berkeley: University of California Press.

Fink, Zera S. (1962). *The Classical Republicans: An Essay in the Recovery of a Pattern of Thought in Seventeenth-Century England.* 2nd ed. Evanston: Northwestern University Press.

Fletcher, Angus. (1971). *The Transcendental Masque: An Essay on Milton's "Comus."* Ithaca: Cornell University Press.

Foucault, Michel. (1972). *The Archeology of Knowledge and the Discourse on Language.* (A. M. Sheridan Smith, trans.). New York: Pantheon Books.

———. (1979). *Discipline and Punish: The Birth of the Prison.* (Alan Sheridan, trans.). New York: Vintage Books.

———. (1973). *The Order of Things: An Archeology of the Human Sciences.* (Richard Howard, trans.). New York: Vintage Books.

———. (1984). "What Is an Author?" (Jouse V. Harari, trans.). In *The Foucault Reader.* (Paul Rabinow, ed.). New York: Pantheon Books, 101–20.

Freud, Sigmund. (1955a). *Beyond the Pleasure Principle* (1920). In *The Standard Edition of the Complete Psychological Works of Sigmund Freud.* (James Strachey, trans. and ed.). Vol. 18. London: Hogarth, 7–64.

———. (1955b). "From the History of An Infantile Neurosis" (1914). In *The Standard Edition of the Complete Psychological Works of Sigmund Freud.* (James Strachey, trans. and ed.). Vol. 17. London: Hogarth, 7–122.

———. (1955c). "Further Remarks on the Neuro-Psychoses of Defence" (1896). In *The Standard Edition of the Complete Psychological Works of Sigmund Freud.* (James Strachey, trans. and ed.). Vol. 3. London: Hogarth, 159–85.

———. (1955d). *The Interpretation of Dreams* (1900). In *The Complete Psychological Works of Sigmund Freud.* (James Strachey, trans. and ed.). Vols. 4 and 5. London: Hogarth.

———. (1955e). "Medusa's Head" (1922). In *The Standard Edition of the Complete Psychological Works of Sigmund Freud.* (James Strachey, trans. and ed.). Vol. 18. London: Hogarth, 273–74.

———. (1955f). "Project for a Scientific Psychology" (1895). In *The Standard Edition of the Complete Psychological Works of Sigmund Freud.* (James Strachey, trans. and ed.). Vol. 1. London: Hogarth, 295–343.

———. (1955g). *Totem and Taboo: Resemblances Between the Psychic Lives of Savages and Neurotics (1913).* In *The Standard Edition of the Complete Psychological Works of Sigmund Freud.* (James Strachey, trans. and ed.). Vol. 13. London: Hogarth, 1–161.

Garber, Marjorie. (1987). "Macbeth: the Male Medusa." in *Shakespeare's Ghost Writers: Literature as Uncanny Causality.* New York: Methuen, 87–123.

George a Greene, the Pinner of Wakefield. (1924). In *Chief Pre-Shakespearean Dramas.* (Joseph Quincy Adams, ed.). Boston: Houghton Mifflin, 691–712.

Gilman, Albert, ed. (1972). "As You Like It." In *The Complete Signet Classic Shakespeare.* New York: Harcourt.

Ginzburg, Carlo. (1980). *The Cheese and the Worms: The Cosmos of a Sixteenth-Century Miller.* (John and Anne Tedeschi, trans.). Harmondsworth: Penguin Books; repr. 1982.

———. (1991). *Ecstacies: Deciphering the Witches' Sabbath.* (Raymond Rosenthal, trans.). New York: Pantheon Books.

Girard, Rene. (1977). *Violence and the Sacred.* (Patrick Gregory, trans.). Baltimore: Johns Hopkins University Press.

Gramsci, Antonio. (1988). *An Antonio Gramsci Reader: Selected Writings, 1916–1935.* (David Forges, ed.). New York: Schocken Books.

Greenblatt, Stephen. (1986). "Psychoanalysis and Renaissance Culture." In *Literary Theory/Renaissance Texts.* (Patricia Parker and David Quint, eds.). Baltimore: Johns Hopkins University Press, 210–24.

———. (1988). "Shakespeare and the Exorcists." In *Shakespearean Negotiations: The Circulation of Social Energy in Renaissance England.* Berkeley: University of California Press, 94–128.

Greene, Thomas M. (1970). "Ben Jonson and the Centered Self." *SEL* 10:325–48.

———. (1982). *Light in Troy: Imitation and Discovery in Renaissance Poetry.* New Haven: Yale University Press.

Guillory, John. (1986). "Dalila's House: *Samson Agonistes* and the Sexual Division of Labor." In *Rewriting the Renaissance: The Discourses of Sexual Difference in Early Modern Europe.* (Margaret W. Ferguson, Maureen Quilligan, and Nancy J. Vickers, eds.). Chicago: University of Chicago Press, 106–22.

Habermas, Jurgen. (1983). "Modernity—An Incomplete Project." In *The Anti-Aesthetic: Essays on Postmodern Culture.* (Hal Foster, ed.). Port Townsend, WA: Bay Press, 3–15.

Halpern, Richard. (1986). "Puritanism and Maenadism in *A Mask.*" In *Rewriting the Renaissance: The Discourses of Sexual Difference in Early Modern Europe.* (Margaret W. Ferguson, Maureen Quilligan, and Nancy J. Vickers, eds.). Chicago: University of Chicago Press, 88–103.

Hartman, Geoffrey. (1970). "'The Nymph Complaining for the Death of Her Faun': A Brief Allegory." In *Beyond Formalism: Literary Essays 1958–1970.* New Haven: Yale University Press, 173–92.

———. (1981). *Saving the Text: Literature/Derrida/Philosophy.* Baltimore: Johns Hopkins University Press.

Havelock, Eric A. (1963). *Preface to Plato.* Cambridge, MA: Harvard University Press.

Hayes, Tom. (1991). "Ben Jonson's Libertine Catholicism." In *Praise Disjoined: Changing Patterns of Salvation in Seventeenth-Century English Literature.* (William P. Shaw, ed.). New York: Peter Lang.

Hayes, Tom, and Lee Quinby. (1989). "The Aporia of Bourgeois Art: Desire in Thomas Mann's *Death in Venice.*" *Criticism* 31:159–77.

Haynes, Jonathan. (1984). "Festivity and the Dramatic Economy of Jonson's *Bartholomew Fair.*" *ELH* 51:645–68.

Hebdige, Dick. (1988). *Hiding in the Light: On Images and Things.* New York: Routledge.

Hedrick, Don K. (1977). "Cooking for the Anthropaphagi: Jonson and His Audience." *SEL* 17:233–45.

Hegel. G. W. F. (1977). *Phenomenology of Spirit.* (A. V. Miller, trans.). Oxford: Oxford University Press.

Heinemann, Margot. (1980). *Puritanism and Theatre: Thomas Middleton and Opposition Drama under the Early Stuarts.* Cambridge: Cambridge University Press.

Helgerson, Richard. (1976). *The Elizabethan Prodigals.* Berkeley: University of California Press.

Herrick, Robert. (1963). *The Complete Poetry of Robert Herrick.* (J. Max Patrick, ed.). New York: Norton; repr. 1968.

Heywood, Thomas, and Richard Brome. (1634). *The Late Lancashire Witches.* London.

Hill, Christopher. (1977). *Milton and the English Revolution.* London: Faber & Faber.

———. (1958). *Puritanism and Revolution: Studies in Interpretation of the English Revolution of the Seventeenth Century.* New York: Schocken Books; repr. 1964.

———. (1967). *Society and Puritanism in Pre-Revolutionary England.* 2nd edn. New York: Schocken Books.

Hillman, James. (1972). *The Myth of Analysis: Three Essays in*

Archetypal Psychology. Evanston: Northwestern University Press.

Hinman, Robert B. (1970). "The Apotheosis of Faust: Poetry and New Philosophy in the Seventeenth Century." In *Metaphysical Poetry.* (Malcolm Bradbury and David Palmer, eds.). Bloomington: Indiana University Press, 149–79.

Holt, J. C. (1989). *Robin Hood.* Rev. ed. London: Thames & Hudson.

Howard, Jean E. (1988). "Crossdressing, The Theatre, and Gender Struggle in Early Modern England." *SQ* 39:418–40.

Hunter, Dianne. (1988). "Doubling, Mythic Difference, and the Scapegoating of Female Power in *Macbeth.*" *The Psychoanalytic Review* 75:127–52.

———. (1985). "Hysteria, Psychoanalysis, and Feminism: The Case of Anna O." In *The (M)other Tongue: Essays in Feminist Psychoanalytic Interpretation.* (Shirley Nelson Garner, Claire Kahane, and Madelon Sprengnether, eds.). Ithaca: Cornell University Press, 89–115.

Ingram, Martin. (1985). "The Reform of Popular Culture? Sex and Marriage in Early Modern England." In *Popular Culture in Seventeenth-Century England.* (Barry Reay, ed.). New York: St. Martin's Press, 129–65.

Irigaray, Luce. (1985). *Speculum of the Other Woman.* (Gillian C. Gill, trans.). Ithaca: Cornell University Press.

James I. (1966). *Daemonologie.* (G. B. Harrison, ed.). New York: Barnes and Noble.

Jorden, Edward. (1603). *A Brief Discourse of a Disease called the Suffocation of the Mother.* London.

Kay, W. David. (1969–70). "The Shaping of Ben Jonson's Career: A Reexamination of Facts and Problems." *MP* 67:224–37.

Keats, John. (1935). *Complete Poetry and Selected Letters.* (James deWitt Thorpe, ed.). New York: Odyssey Press.

Keen, Maurice. (1961). *The Outlaws of Medieval Legend.* Toronto: University of Toronto Press.

Knapp, Peggy. (1979). "Ben Jonson and the Publicke Riot." *ELH* 46:577–94.

Knights, L. C. (1937). *Drama and Society in the Age of Jonson.* Harmondsworth: Penguin Books; repr. 1962.

Lacan, Jacques. (1977). "The Agency of the Letter in the Unconscious or Reason Since Freud." In *Écrits: A Selection.* (Alan Sheridan, trans.). New York: Norton, 146–78.

———. (1968). "The Function of Language." In *Speech and Language in Psychoanalysis.* (Anthony Wilden, trans.). Baltimore: Johns Hopkins University Press, 3–87.

———. (1982). "Guiding Remarks for a Congress on Feminine

Sexuality." (Jacqueline Rose, trans.). In *Feminine Sexuality: Jacques Lacan and the école freudienne.* (Juliet Mitchell and Jacqueline Rose, eds.). New York: Norton, 86–98.

LaCapra, Dominick. (1989). *Soundings in Critical Theory.* Ithaca: Cornell University Press.

Lachmann, Renate. (1988–89). "Bakhtin and Carnival." *Cultural Critique* No. 11:115–54.

Lang, Berel. (1986). "Postmodernism in Philosophy: Nostalgia for the Future, Waiting for the Past." *NLH* 18:208–23.

Larner, Christina. (1984). *Witchcraft and Religion: The Politics of Popular Belief.* (Alan Macfarlane, ed.). New York: Basil Blackwell.

Lasch, Christopher. (1984). "The Politics of Nostalgia: Losing History in the Mists of Ideology." *Harper's* (November), 65–70.

Leavis, F. R. (1959). *Revaluation: Tradition and Development in English Poetry.* London: Chatto and Windus.

Le Roy Ladurie, Emmanuel. (1974). *The Peasants of Languedoc.* (John Day, trans.). Urbana: University of Illinois Press.

Levin, Harry. (1969). *The Myth of the Golden Age in the Renaissance.* Bloomington: Indiana University Press.

Levine, Laura. (1986). "Men in Women's Clothing: Anti–theatricality and Effeminization from 1579 to 1642." *Criticism* 28:121–43.

Lindley, David. (1986). "Embarrassing Ben: The Masques for Frances Howard." *ELR* 16:343–59.

Loewenstein, Joseph. (1984). *Responsive Readings: Versions of Echo in Pastoral, Epic, and the Jonsonian Masque.* New Haven: Yale University Press.

Low, Anthony. (1985). *The Georgic Revolution,* Princeton: Princeton University Press.

Lucan. (1957). *Pharsalia.* (Robert Graves, trans.). Baltimore: Penguin Books.

MacCabe, Colin. (1986). "Defining Popular Culture." In *High Theory/Low Culture: Analysing Popular Television and Film.* (Colin MacCabe, ed.). New York: St. Martin's Press, 1–10.

MacCannell, Juliet Flower. (1983). "Oedipus Wrecks: Lacan, Stendhal, and the Narrative Form of the Real." In *Lacan and Narration: The Psychoanalytic Difference in Narrative Theory.* (Robert Con Davis, ed.). Baltimore: Johns Hopkins University Press, 910–40.

Mahood, M. M. (1949). *Poetry and Humanism.* New York: Norton; repr. 1970.

Mann, Thomas. (1954). *Death in Venice and Seven Other Stories.* (H. T. Lowe-Porter, trans.). New York: Vintage Books.

Marcus, Leah S. (1986). *The Politics of Mirth: Jonson, Herrick, Milton, Marvell, and the Defense of Old Holiday Pastimes.* Chicago: University of Chicago Press.

Marotti, Arthur F. (1972). "All About Ben Jonson's Poetry." *ELH* 39:208–37.

Marvell, Andrew. (1971). *The Poems and Letters of Andrew Marvell.* (H. M. Margoliouth, ed.); 3rd edn. (rev. Pierre Legouis). 2 vols. Oxford: Clarendon Press.

McGann, Tara. (1989). "Desire Before the Law: Being an Examination of the Ideological Category and Psychical Mechanisms of the Diabolic in Sixteenth- and Seventeenth-Century France." Unpublished essay.

McLuskie, Kathleen. (1989). *Renaissance Dramatists.* Atlantic Highlands: Humanities Press International.

Middleton, Thomas. (1964). *The Witch.* In *The Works of Thomas Middleton.* (A. H. Bullen, ed.). Vol. 5. New York: AMS Press, 351–453.

Miller, J. Hillis. (1985). "The Critic as Host." In *Deconstruction and Criticism.* New York: Continuum, 217–53.

Montrose, Louis Adrian. (1983). "Of Gentlemen and Shepherds: The Politics of Elizabethan Pastoral Form." *ELH* 50:415–59.

Moran, Jo Ann Hoeppner. (1985). *The Growth of English Schooling, 1340–1548: Learning, Literacy, and Laicization in Pre-Reformation York Diocese.* Princeton: Princeton University Press.

Morris, Meaghan. (1988). "Tooth and Claw: Tales of Survival and *Crocodile Dundee.*" In *Universal Abandon: The Politics of Postmodernism.* (Andrew Ross, ed.). Minneapolis: University of Minnesota Press, 105–27.

Morton, A. L. (1969). *The English Utopia.* London: Lawrence & Wishart.

Muchembled, Robert. (1985). *Popular Culture and Elite Culture in France 1400–1750.* (Lydia Cochrane, trans.). Baton Rouge, LA: Louisiana State University Press.

Munday, Anthony. (1580). *A Second and Third Blast of Retrait from Plays and Theatres.* London.

Murray, Margaret. (1921). *The Witch-Cult in Western Europe.* Oxford: Clarendon Press; repr. 1971.

Murray, Timothy. (1987). *Theatrical Legitimation: Allegories of Genius in Seventeenth-Century England and France.* New York: Oxford University Press.

Newton, Richard C. (1982). "Jonson and the (Re-)Invention of the Book." In *Classic and Cavalier: Essays on Jonson and the Sons of Ben.* (Claude J. Summers and Ted-Larry Pebworth, eds.). Pittsburgh: University of Pittsburgh Press, 31–55.

Nietzsche, Friedrich. (1967a). *The Birth of Tragedy* and *The Case of Wagner.* (Walter Kaufmann, trans.). New York: Vintage Books.

——. (1967b). *On the Genealogy of Morals* and *Ecce Homo.* (Walter Kaufmann, trans.). New York: Vintage Books; repr. 1989.

Norbrook, David. (1984). *Poetry and Politics in the English Renaissance.* Boston: Routledge and Kegan Paul.

Onat, Etta Soiref, ed. (1980). William Rowley, Thomas Dekker, John Ford, *The Witch of Edmonton: A Critical Edition.* New York: Garland.

Ong, Walter J., S.J. (1977). *Interfaces of the Word: Studies in the Evolution of Consciousness and Culture.* Ithaca: Cornell University Press.

Orgel, Stephen. (1965). *The Jonsonian Masques.* Cambridge, MA: Harvard University Press.

Palmer, Robert. (1990). "Dark Metal: Not Just Smash and Trash." *The New York Times.* Arts and Leisure Section. (Sunday, November 4), 31.

Parry, Graham. (1981). *The Golden Age Restored: The Culture of the Stuart Court, 1603–42.* New York: St. Martin's Press; repr. 1985.

Partridge, Edward B. (1958). *The Broken Compass: A Study of the Major Comedies of Ben Jonson.* Cambridge, MA: Harvard University Press.

Patterson, Annabel. (1987). *Pastoral and Ideology: Virgil to Valery.* Berkeley: University of California Press.

Pecheux, Michel. (1982). *Language, Semantics and Ideology: Stating the Obvious.* (Harbans Nagpal, trans.). New York: St. Martin's Press.

Peterson, Richard S. (1981). *Imitation and Praise in the Poems of Ben Jonson.* New Haven: Yale University Press.

Post, Jonathan F. S. (1982). *Henry Vaughan: The Unfolding Vision.* Princeton: Princeton University Press.

Puig, Manuel. (1980). *Kiss of the Spider Woman.* (Thomas Colchie, trans.). New York: Vintage Books.

Putnam, Michael C. J. (1982). "Horace C.3.30: The Lyricist as Hero." In *Essays on Latin Lyric, Elegy, and Epic.* Princeton: Princeton University Press, 133–51.

Quint, David. (1986). "Introduction." In *Literary Theory/Renaissance Texts.* (Patricia Parker and David Quint, eds.). Baltimore: Johns Hopkins University Press, 1–19.

Randall, Dale B. J. (1975). *Jonson's Gypsies Unmasked: Background and Theme of The Gypsies Metamorphos'd.* Durham: Duke University Press.

Reiss, Timothy. (1982). *The Discourse of Modernism*. Ithaca: Cornell University Press.

Rigby, Peter. (1985). *Persistent Pastoralists: Nomadic Societies in Transition*. London: Zed Books.

Riggs, David. (1989). *Ben Jonson: A Life*. Cambridge, MA: Harvard University Press.

Ross, Andrew. (1989). *No Respect: Intellectuals and Popular Culture*. New York: Routledge.

Saunders, David, and Ian Hunter. (1991). "Lessons from the 'Literatory': How to Historicize Authorship." *CritI* 17:479–509.

Scot, Reginald. (1930). *The Discoverie of Witchcraft* (1584). New York: Dover; repr. 1972.

Segal, Charles. (1982). *Dionysiac Poetics and Euripides' "Bacchae."* Princeton: Princeton University Press.

Shakespeare, William. (1972). *The Complete Signet Classic Shakespeare*. (Sylvan Barnet, ed.). New York: Harcourt.

Shepherd, Simon. (1981). *Amazons and Warrior Women: Varieties of Feminism in Seventeenth-Century Drama*. New York: St. Martin's Press.

Simeone, W. E. (1951). "The May Games and the Robin Hood Legend." *Journal of American Folklore* 64:265–74.

Spenser, Edmund. (1912). *Poetical Works*. (J. C. Smith and E. de Selincourt, eds.). London: Oxford University Press.

Stallybrass, Peter, and Allon White. (1986). *The Politics and Poetics of Transgression*. Ithaca: Cornell University Press.

Stallybrass, Peter. (1986). "Patriarchal Territories: The Body Enclosed." In *Rewriting the Renaissance: The Discourses of Sexual Difference in Early Modern Europe*. (Margaret W. Ferguson, Maureen Quilligan, and Nancy J. Vickers, eds.). Chicago: University of Chicago Press, 123–42.

———. (1985). " 'Drunk with the cup of liberty': Robin Hood, the carnivalesque, and the rhetoric of violence in early modern England." *Semiotica* 54.1–2:113–45.

Stewart, Susan. (1984). *On Longing: Narratives of the Miniature, the Gigantic, the Souvenier, the Collection*. Baltimore: Johns Hopkins University Press.

Stone, Lawrence. (1979). *The Family, Sex, and Marriage in England 1500–1800*. Abridged ed. New York: Harper & Row.

Stroud, Theodore A. (1947). "Ben Jonson and Father Thomas Wright." *ELH* 14:274–82.

Swinburne, Algernon Charles. (1889). *A Study of Ben Jonson*. London.

Thomas, Keith. (1971). *Religion and the Decline of Magic*. London: Weidenfeld and Nicolson.

Thomas, P. W. (1973). "Two Cultures? Court and Country Under

Charles I." In *The Origins of the English Civil War*. (Conrad Russell, ed.). New York: Barnes and Noble, 168–93.

Tonkin, Humphrey. (1972). *Spenser's Courteous Pastoral: Book Six of the Faerie Queene*. Oxford: Clarendon Press.

Underdown, David. (1985). *Revel, Riot, and Rebellion: Popular Politics and Culture in England 1603–1660*. Oxford: Clarendon Press.

Urban, Raymond. (1975). "The Somerset Affair, the Belvoir Witches, and Jonson's Pastoral Comedies." *Harvard Library Bulletin* 23:295–323.

Vaughan, Henry. (1964). *The Complete Poetry of Henry Vaughan*. (French Fogle, ed.). New York: Doubleday Anchor.

Venuti, Lawrence. (1989). *Our Halcyon Dayes: English Prerevolutionary Texts and Postmodern Culture*. Madison: University of Wisconsin Press.

Vernant, Jean–Pierre. (1965). *Mythe et Pensee les Grecs*. Paris: F. Maspero.

Virgil, (1972). *The Aeneid*. (Allen Mandelbaum, trans.). New York: Bantam Books.

[Waldron, F. G., ed.]. (1783). *The Sad Shepherd*. London.

Walker, D. P. (1981). *Unclean Spirits: Possession and Exorcism in France and England in the Late Sixteenth and Early Seventeenth Centuries*. Philadelphia: University of Pennsylvania Press.

Wayne, Don E. (1982). "*Drama and Society in the Age of Jonson: An Alternative View*." *RD* 13:103–37.

———. (1984). *Penshurst: The Semiotics of Place and the Poetics of History*. Madison: University of Wisconsin Press.

Weed, Elizabeth, ed. (1989). *Coming To Terms: Feminism, Theory, Politics*. New York: Routledge.

Weimann, Robert. (1983). " 'Appropriation' and Modern History in Renaissance Prose Narrative." *NLH* 14:459–95.

———. (1978). *Shakespeare and the Popular Tradition in the Theater: Studies in the Social Dimension of Dramatic Form and Function*. (Robert Schwartz, trans. and ed.). Baltimore: Johns Hopkins University Press.

———. (1988). "Text, Author-Function, and Appropriation in Modern Narrative: Toward a Sociology of Representation." *CritI* 14:431–47.

Weinberg, Florence M. (1972). *The Wine and the Will: Rabelais' Bacchic Christianity*. Detroit: Wayne State University Press.

Wesling, Donald. (1981). "Difficulties of the Bardic." *CritI* 8:69–81.

White, Beatrice. (1965). *Cast of Ravens: The Strange Case of Sir Thomas Overbury*. London: John Murray.

Wilden, Anthony. (1968). "Lacan and the Discourse of the Other."

In Jacques Lacan, *Speech and Language in Psychoanalysis.* (Anthony Wilden, trans.). Baltimore: Johns Hopkins University Press, 157–311.

Wiles, David. (1981). *The Early Plays of Robin Hood.* Cambridge: D. S. Brewer.

Williams, Raymond. (1973). *The Country and the City.* New York: Oxford University Press.

Wiltenburg, Robert. (1989). *Ben Jonson and Self-Love: The Subtlest Maze of All.* Columbia: University of Missouri Press.

Wittreich, Joseph. (1984). "'Image of that horror': the Apocalypse in *King Lear.*" In *The Apocalypse in English Renaissance Thought and Literature.* (C. A. Patrides and Joseph Wittreich, eds.). Ithaca: Cornell University Press, 175–206.

Woodbridge, Linda. (1984). *Women and the English Renaissance: Literature and the Nature of Womankind, 1540–1620.* Urbana: University of Illinois Press.

Womack, Peter. (1986). *Ben Jonson.* London: Basil Blackwell.

The Wonderfull Discoverie of the Witch-crafts of Margaret and Philip Flower . . . . (1619). London.

Yates, Frances A. (1975). *Shakespeare's Last Plays: A New Approach.* London: Routledge.

Index

About the Author

TOM HAYES is professor of English at Baruch College and The Graduate Center, City University of New York. Dr. Hayes earned his Ph.D. from New York University, and was the recipient of an NEH Fellowship in 1980–81. Widely published in scholarly journals, his publications also include *Winstanley the Digger* (Harvard University Press, 1979).